T0311769

# The Executive's Guide to AI and Analytics

# The Executive's Guide to AI and Analytics

## The Foundations of Execution and Success in the New World

Scott Burk, PhD and Gary D. Miner, PhD

Routledge
Taylor & Francis Group

A PRODUCTIVITY PRESS BOOK

First published 2022
by Routledge
605 Third Avenue, New York, NY 10158

and by Routledge
4 Park Square, Milton Park, Abingdon, Oxon, OX14 4RN

*Routledge is an imprint of the Taylor & Francis Group, an informa business*

© 2022 Scott Burk & Gary D. Miner

*Library of Congress Cataloging-in-Publication Data*
A catalog record for this title has been requested

ISBN: 9781032007953 (hbk)
ISBN: 9781032007946 (pbk)
ISBN: 9781003175759 (ebk)

DOI: 10.4324/9781003175759

Typeset in Garamond
by Deanta Global Publishing Services, Chennai, India

To my wife Jackie, you are a rock star!
Thanks for all your support!

Scott Burk

To my wife, Linda, for putting up with my book writing
activities, when we are "supposed" to be retired, doing
what "retired people usually do" – travel and forget about
their professional lives!!! … But did I not say "this will
be the last book!" … when in fact we have three more
to go, Linda herself being lead author of the 2nd edition
of our "big medical book" with expected publication
date within a year – *then* we can *really retire*, right?

Gary D. Miner

# Contents

# Authors

**Scott Burk** has been solving complex business and health-care problems for 25 years, through science, statistics, machine learning, and business acumen. Scott started his career, well actually, in analytics, as an Analytic Chemist after graduating with a double major in Biology and Chemistry from Texas State University. He continued his education, going to school at night and taking advanced courses in science and math at the University of Texas at Dallas (UTD). He then started programming at the toxicology lab where he was working and thus started taking computer science (CS) and business courses until he graduated with a Master's in Business with a concentration in finance soon after.

Texas Instruments (TI) hired him as a financial systems analyst in Semiconductor Group, but due to TI's needs and Scott's love of computers, he soon became a systems analyst for corporate TI. He worked there for three years and started itching to get back to school (even though he continued to take courses at night [Operations Research and CS] through TI's generous educational program). TI granted him an educational leave of absence and he went to Baylor University to teach in the business school and get a PhD in Statistics. He joined Baylor as a non-tenure track professor teaching Quantitative Business Analysis (today = business analytics).

After graduating, Scott went back to TI as a Decision Support Manager for the consumer arm of TI (today called consulting data scientist). Here he engaged in many functional areas – marketing and sales, finance, engineering, logistics, customer relations, the call center, and more. It was a dream job, but unfortunately, TI exited that business.

Scott joined Scott and White, a large integrated health-care delivery system in Texas as a consulting statistician. He moved into an executive role as Associate Executive Director, Information Systems, leading Data Warehousing, Business Intelligence, and Quality Organizations working with clinics, hospitals, and the health plan. At the same time, he received a faculty appointment and taught informatics with Texas A&M University. He left, but later came back to Baylor, Scott and White (BSW) as Chief Statistician for BSW Health Plan.

Scott continued his education, getting an advanced management certification from Southern Methodist University (SMU) and Master's degree (MS) in Data Mining (machine learning) from Central Connecticut State University. Scott is a firm believer in lifelong learning.

He also worked as Chief Statistician at Overstock, reengineering the way they tested and evaluated marketing campaigns and other programs (analytics, statistics). He launched their "total customer value" program. He was a Lead Pricing Scientist (analytics, optimization) for a B2B pricing optimization company (Zilliant) for a number of years. He thoroughly enjoyed working with a rich, diverse, well-educated group that affected the way he looks at multidisciplinary methods of solving problems.

He was a Risk Manager for eBay/Paypal identifying fraud and other risks on the platform and payment system. He has been working the last few years supporting software development, marketing, and sales, specifically data infrastructure, data science, and analytics platforms, for Dell and now TIBCO. He supports his desire to learn and keep current by writing and teaching in the Masters of Data Science Program at City University of New York.

**Gary D. Miner** earned his BS from Hamline University, St. Paul, MN, with Biology, Chemistry, and Education as majors; his MS in Zoology and Population Genetics from the University of Wyoming; and his PhD in Biochemical Genetics from the University of Kansas as the recipient of a NASA Pre-Doctoral Fellowship. During the doctoral study years, he also studied mammalian genetics at The Jackson Laboratory, Bar Harbor, ME, under a College Training Program on an NIH award; and another College Training Program at the Bermuda Biological Station, St. George's West, Bermuda in a Marine Developmental Embryology Course, on an NSF award; and a third College Training Program held at the University of California, San Diego, at the Molecular Techniques in Developmental Biology Institute, again on an NSF award.

Following that he studied as a postdoctoral student at the University of Minnesota in Behavioral Genetics, where, along with research in schizophrenia and Alzheimer's Disease (AD), he learned "how to write books" from assisting in editing two book manuscripts of his mentor, Irving Gottesman, PhD (Dr. Gottesman returned the favor 41 years later by writing two tutorials for this *Practical Text Mining* book). After academic research and teaching positions, Gary did another two-year NIH-postdoctoral in Psychiatric Epidemiology and Biostatistics at the University of Iowa where he became thoroughly immersed in studying affective disorders and Alzheimer's Disease. Altogether he spent over 30 years researching and writing papers and books on the genetics of Alzheimer's Disease (Miner, G.D., Richter, R, Blass, J.P., Valentine, J.L, and Winters-Miner, Linda, *Familial Alzheimer's Disease: Molecular Genetics and Clinical Perspectives*, Dekker: NYC, 1989; and Miner, G.D., Winters-Miner, Linda, Blass, J.P., Richter, R, and Valentine, J.L., *Caring for Alzheimer's Patients: A Guide for*

*Family & Healthcare Providers*, Plenum Press Insight Books: NYC, 1989).

Over the years he held positions, including professor and chairman of a department, at various universities, including the University of Kansas, the University of Minnesota, Northwest Nazarene University, Eastern Nazarene University, Southern Nazarene University, and Oral Roberts University Medical School, where he was Associate Professor of Pharmacology and Director of the Alzheimer Disease and Geriatric Disorders Research Laboratories. For a period of time in the 1990s, he was also a visiting Clinical Professor of Psychology for Geriatrics at the Fuller Graduate School of Psychology and Fuller Theological Seminary in Pasadena, CA.

In 1985, he and his wife, Dr. Linda Winters-Miner (author of several tutorials in this book), founded The Familial Alzheimer's Disease Research Foundation (also known as "The Alzheimer's Foundation"), which became a leading force in organizing both local and international scientific meetings and thus bringing together all the leaders in the field of genetics of AD from several countries, which then led to the writing of the first scientific book on the genetics of AD; this book included papers by over 100 scientists who participated in the First International Symposium on the Genetics of Alzheimer's Disease held in Tulsa, OK, in October 1987. During this time, he was also an Affiliate Research Scientist with the Oklahoma Medical Research Foundation located in Oklahoma City with the University of Oklahoma School of Medicine.

Gary was influential in bringing all of the world's leading scientists working on genetics of AD together at just the right time, when various laboratories from Harvard to Duke University and University of California-San Diego, to the University of Heidelberg, in Germany, and universities in Belgium, France, England, and Perth, Australia, were beginning to find "genes" which they thought were related to Alzheimer's Disease.

During the 1990s, Gary was appointed to the Oklahoma Governor's Task Force on Alzheimer's Disease, and was also Associate Editor for Alzheimer's Disease for the *Journal of Geriatric Psychiatry & Neurology*, which he still serves on to this day. By 1995, most of these dominantly inherited genes for AD had been discovered, and the one that Gary had been working on since the mid-1980s with the University of Washington in Seattle was the last of these initial five to be identified – this gene on Chromosome 1 of the human genome. At that time, having met the goal of finding out some of the genetics of AD, Gary decided to do something different, to find an area of the business world, and since he had been analyzing data for over 30 years, working for StatSoft, Inc. as a Senior Statistician and Data Mining Consultant seemed a perfect "semi-retirement" career. Interestingly (as his wife had predicted), he discovered that the "business world" was much more fun than the "academic world", and at a KDD-Data Mining meeting in 1999 in San Francisco, he decided that he would specialize in "data mining". Incidentally, he first met Bob Nisbet there who told him, "You just have to meet this bright young rising star John Elder!", and within minutes Bob found John introduced me to him, as he was also at this meeting.

As Gary delved into this new "data mining" field and looked at statistics textbooks in general, he saw the need for "practical statistical books" and so started writing chapters and organizing various outlines for different books. Gary, Bob, and John kept running into each other at KDD meetings, and eventually at a breakfast meeting in Seattle in August 2005 decided that they need to write a book on data mining, and right there reorganized Gary's outline which eventually became the book *Handbook of Statistical Analysis and Data Mining Applications* (published in 2009 by Elsevier). And then, in 2012, he was the lead author of a second book *Practical Text Mining* (published by Elsevier/Academic Press).

And then came a third in this "series" in 2015: *Practical Predictive Analytics* and *Decisioning Systems for Medicine*. All thanks to Dr. Irving Gottesman, Gary's "mentor in book writing", who planted the seed back in 1970 while Gary was doing a postdoctoral with him at the University of Minnesota.

His latest book was released in 2018, the second edition of *Handbook of Statistical Analysis* (published in 2009) and *Data Mining Applications*. His book *Healthcare's Out Sick – Predicting a Cure – Solutions that Work!!!* is written more for the layperson and decision-maker. It was published in 2019 by Routledge/Taylor & Francis Group.

Gary is currently finishing the 2nd Edition of *Practical Data Analytics for Innovation in Medicine: Bringing Person-Centered & Patient-Directed Healthcare To the World*, publication date late in 2022 by Elsevier-Academic Press; and is also working on a second and third book in the *It's All Analytics* series with Scott Burk, PhD. He also teaches courses periodically in "Predictive Analytics and Healthcare Analytics" at the University of California-Irvine.

# Chapter 1

# Introduction: Sources of Failure

> In any given moment we have two options: to step forward into growth or to step back into safety.
>
> What one can be, one must be!
>
> **– Abraham Maslow**

Where is the artificial intelligence (AI) and analytics revolution? We often hear miraculous stories of cutting-edge breakthroughs. It started with IBM's Watson's defeat against champions Brad Rutter and Ken Jennings in Jeopardy ten years ago for $1M. Six years ago, the AlphaGo was the first computer to beat a professional Go player, Fan Hill.

If you listen or read the news, you will hear stories of the miraculous wonders of AI and analytics; how they are changing the world. From this you would think that companies across the globe are achieving miraculous results, right? From LinkedIn to whitepapers, from national news outlets and syndicated news

> IBM's Watson has been plagued with failure and lawsuits. In 2017 AlphaGo was retired.

DOI: 10.4324/9781003175759-1

to blogs, AI and analytics have been hot stories for years. Programs are now mature and successful, right?

Not so much. We don't get the full picture. We don't read the unwritten story. We read what is available and what is available is meant to sensationalize the stories of the practice. It turns out a large number of AI and analytics programs are not living up to expectations, a number are sick or dying.

**Is investment lacking?** No. Companies now are spending more than ever on data, analytics, and AI technologies. AI investment in the United States is growing 36% per year, and it is growing faster in some other countries with China growing over 300%. In healthcare, 74% of executives said their organizations would invest more in predictive modeling in 2021.

**Is it lack of technology?** No. There are fascinating breakthroughs occurring on all fronts with image, voice, and streaming pattern recognition at the forefront. These technologies are driving investment and leading many initiatives, with applications from radiology to autonomous vehicles.

**Is it lack of technical talent?** Not really. While some studies cite that we need to train more data scientists, developers, and related professionals, the curve of demand by supply is dampening. And, some experts are suggesting the increasing popularity of data scientists may cause an oversupply of talent.

**Is it lack of creating an executable strategic plan?** While there has been a lot of strategic wishing, organizations lack meaningful strategic plans – specifically, **the development of executable strategies and the leadership to see these strategies brought to fruition**. This is the missing element. The critical element that many organizations lack.

You hear and read the success stories, but these are not indicative of the journey most companies face. What you **don't hear or read is**:

- **The majority of companies are failing** with over three-quarters of their big data and AI initiatives remaining a challenge.
- **Over half of organizations** state that they are "**not yet treating data as a business asset**".
- **Over half of organizations** admit that they are **not competing on data and analytics**.
- Seven out of ten companies (70%) in a 2020 MIT study reported minimal or no impact from AI so far. Among the 90% of companies that have made some investment in AI, fewer than two out of five (only 40%) report business gains from AI in the past three years.
- According to New Vantage Partners Big Data and AI Executive Survey 2021, **only about 25% of organizations have actually forged this data-driven culture**:

  This year's findings exhibit that challenge to an even greater degree. All questions relating to the long-term progress of corporate data initiatives exhibited declines from 2019 and 2020 levels, a disappointing development.

Those companies that have digitally transformed themselves are 26% more profitable than their average industry competitors. But this has required an investment in leadership as well as in technology. Research across the five global industrial revolutions point out one common element of companies that were successful versus those that were not – **top leadership was involved at every level of the organization and this leadership firmly focused on success**.

> Eisenhower said, "Leadership is the art of getting people to want to do, what must be done".

There are stories about companies investing in amazing technology, and such might be true, but that is not where organizations are failing. **Over 93% of businesses report their people and processes are the problem, not technology**.

You will find dozens of books on AI and analytics technology. You will find dozens on the theory and applications of AI and analytics techniques. You will even find dozens more written for data scientists and practitioners of the trade. What you will **not** find is many books that offer leadership and management, and the candid truth of where organizations are failing and how to overcome these gaps and challenges. You will not find stories of failure and why failure occurred.

Whether you have a mature AI and analytics program, whether you are just starting your program, or whether you have had some success or not, there is a way to be successful in your data-driven journey. There is a way to drive results and return on investment.

Too often analytics strategic planning is done without regard to the plan for execution. Often it is done by a small isolated contingent of leaders without involving necessary design teams, business units, and distributed leaders. Thus, too often, the analytics program suffers. This is not due to lack of investment, but rather due to lack of proper planning for **alignment** of **technical systems**, **work processes**, **social systems**, and **behavioral systems** to achieve business strategy.

By 2022, it is estimated that 90% of corporate strategies will explicitly mention information (data) as a critical enterprise asset and analytics as an essential competency.

It is critical that organizations get this right.

We are in an AI and analytics revolution. **Organizations must successfully plan and align and then execute**. They also need to build into their plans the ability to adapt quickly to external as well as internal forces. If they do this, they should thrive. If they don't, they will likely not survive.

## A MODERN-DAY STORY AND
## THE NEED TO ADAPT

She addressed the board of directors. She had been preparing for days. In fact, her brightest minds had been preparing for days. This was not going to be a typical meeting. That was evident from the last board meeting coupled with several one-on-one conversations with several board members. She had to successfully defend her position or she was out of a job.

She was Tricia Garcia and she was the CEO of South State Medical, a medium-size nonprofit medical system with seven hospitals, various facilities, and over two million outpatient visits per year. She followed a ten-year rise and had been at the top for the last three years. She was a shining star, but now she might be a falling one.

The problem? The board had brought her on with a limited set of business initiatives (expand the network, cost containment, and the like). But, most importantly, they wanted her to launch an AI and analytics program. Board members were well read and some had experience with the power of data-driven initiatives. They could not understand her failures.

Susan was not alone. Despite all of the hype around analytics at conferences, from consultants, from software companies, and from marketing engines, analytics are not living up to expectations in the majority of organizations. AI and analytics have been far from successful. In fact, over three-quarters of AI analytics projects never run successfully in operations. Investment in infrastructure is markedly up, staffing is markedly up, and dozens of new master's degree programs are available at top universities. Mainstream news channels have been advocating the allure, the excitement of it all, for some time. We have heard "we need to be data-driven" for years. Why aren't we more successful?

Susan's board is not uncommon. A majority of organizations (57%) believe that AI technology will substantially transform their company within the next three years **with the window for competitive differentiation with AI quickly closing.**[*] With leaders increasingly seeing AI as helping to drive the next great economic expansion, a fear of missing out is spreading around the industry.

There will be many more presentations like Susan's in the coming years as boards push on CEOs to start new programs or turn around their AI and analytics lackluster results.

While some companies are not successfully executing their programs, there are companies that are very successful; the gaps are startling. Companies successfully competing on AI and analytics will clearly win out in their industries. In fact, according to Deloitte in a study, the gaps between ROI Overperformers Underperformers (Deloitte's terms) showed a 60–80% gap that varied across industry.

> "Seventy percent of strategic failures are due to poor execution of leadership, not for lack of smarts or vision". – Ram Charan

Therefore, these data-driven programs will only accelerate; organizations that are successful in delivering these programs will survive and those that are not will most likely perish. **The keys to success are the right leadership, accelerated adaptation, and execution.**

---

[*] https://www2.deloitte.com/us/en/insights/focus/cognitive-technologies/ai-investment-by-country.html

This is especially true in a post-COVID world. COVID has brought about many changes:

- How industries and markets are structured and how they operate
- How people work
- The need for more automated actions
- Quick, agile, and intelligent decision-making augmented by analytics

The evidence is clear. There are organizations that have successfully implemented AI and analytics programs. There are organizations that have not. Only those that can achieve data-driven success will survive. We started this discussion with two Maslow quotes that we think are applicable:

> In any given moment we have two options: to step forward into growth or to step back into safety.

> What one can be, one must be!

We hope your organization will step forward into the AI and analytics revolution and be all that it can be.

# Chapter 2

# AI and Analytics Failure and How to Overcome It

Having a vision for what you want is not enough.
Vision without execution is hallucination.

**– Thomas A. Edison**

No excuses. No explanation. You don't win on emotion. You win on execution.

**– Tony Dungy**

This executive guide addresses the fundamentals of people, culture, strategy, and execution for leaders and decision-makers. Getting these fundamentals wrong makes for the primary gaps between having an artificial intelligence (AI) and analytics program that fails and having a successful AI and analytics program. Two of these – people and culture – are part of what we call the six foundations, as illustrated in Figure 2.1. We have written about the other four foundations elsewhere and they are typically not associated with the root cause of failure of AI programs. We dive a bit deeper into the six foundations

DOI: 10.4324/9781003175759-2

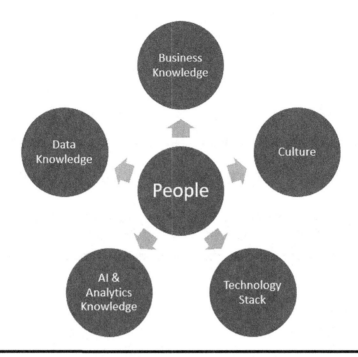

**Figure 2.1   The six foundations of the success of AI and analytics programs.**

in Chapter 3 and provide references. For now, we dive into the key reasons for program failure.

Leaders have two principal jobs:

1. Developing a strategy
2. Executing the strategy

That's it.

What needs to be done? Create a plan – strategy. Make the plan reality – exe-

> "Strategy defines and communicates an organizations unique position, and says that it should determine how organizational resources, skills and competencies should be combined to create competitive advantages".
> – Michael Porter

cution. Yes, there are many other jobs that leaders undertake, but there are no more important jobs than strategy development and making that strategy happen.

Which one of these is taught in business school? Which one of these are most books written about? Which is sexier? Which one of these is applauded by the press and other media? **Developing strategy**. Which is the hardest? **Executing strategy!** That is the reason organizations are failing. They are not executing!

The root cause of failure in AI and analytics programs is a lack of execution. As we stated in the introduction, developing a successful AI and analytics program is not an option. It is a requirement that organizations are failing to deliver successfully upon. Why? Organizations are investing the money; they have the right technology, and the technical talent. What they are lacking is leadership. Organizations need leaders that can "develop plans to execute" and then "execute the plans".

When companies fail to deliver on their promises, the most frequent explanation is that leadership's strategy was wrong. However, the strategy itself is not often the cause. Strategies often fail because they aren't executed well. And they aren't executed well because one part of the strategy was poorly constructed: most of the emphasis focused on the "what we want to do" part of strategy, and little if any focused on the "how will we do it". The question of "how we will do it" is missing.

Sure, it is great to be part of the executive leadership. It is fun to be in the inner circle; it is a powerful feeling to be in the elite club. For this reason, decisions are often made in isolation among the executive leadership team without input from the broader organization. High-level milestones, made by the elite few with lofty, nonspecific strategies based on revenue growth, increased market share, margin growth, or cost reduction. Moreover, corporate campaigns like diversity, social responsibility, work–life balance, and employee health. Because these strategies are made by the select/elite few, they often do not get executed successfully, deep within the organization.

**LACK OF "EXECUTION" IN BUSINESS SCHOOLS
AND THE BUSINESS VERNACULAR**

Execution is not often expressed as a term in business, if people talk about it at all. For all the concern about it in other aspects of society, hardly anybody in business really knows what it is. It may be described as "it's getting things done. It is about operations rather than generating ideas and planning". They may say "it is meeting objectives or goals". If we ask for specifics on "how do you execute to get things done", the dialogue goes rapidly downhill. Whether they're students or senior executives, it's soon clear – to them as well as to us – they don't have the foggiest idea what it means to execute. And why should they? It is not part of the everyday business vernacular. There is not an "Execution" MBA class. There are few books written on execution.

"Education without execution is extinction". – Bo Sanchez

An AI and analytics program is a vital part of a broader business strategy. It cannot be considered an adjunct, specialized program, or a popular corporate campaign. AI and analytics must be enmeshed in every part of the broader strategy. Your strategy will be specific to your organization, and the way you integrate the AI and analytics program must be specific to your business initiatives. However, this strategy cannot be created in isolation by the executive leadership team.

# What Is Execution and Why Is It Important?

Execution is taking a plan or strategy and "getting it done". Execution is the force that drives AI and analytics to success from the boardroom, through all organizational functions, and into all customer expectations. The leadership team has to drive the message through the entire organization. They have to be the consistent voice. Belief is important to outcome, and leaders create the belief. They have to develop the business strategy around AI and analytics and impart the belief that AI and analytics are the bridge to success. They have to effectively "operationalize" this strategy. They have to work intimately with every manager and staff member to make it happen – to execute. We therefore must focus on the tenets of execution.

> "Leadership versus Management"

## A NOTE ON LEADERSHIP VERSUS MANAGEMENT

We will be speaking a great deal on leadership and management, of leaders and managers. What is the difference? Leadership is primarily about strategy and planning; plotting the course for the organization. Management is about running the organization. Management is more tactical.

Leadership is about **effectiveness**. Management is about **efficiency**.

Stephen Covey provides a great example where workers are plowing through a jungle with machetes. Management's role is to make sure that everyone is up to date with the latest machete-wielding techniques. Management makes sure everyone has the proper nutrition, the proper equipment, and the machetes are razor sharp. This is **efficiency**.

Leadership is about climbing a tree, making a realization, and shouting – "wrong jungle!" This is **strategy**.

You can be efficient doing the wrong thing.

## Execution Is Integral to Strategy

Execution is a discipline. It is a practice; it needs to become a habit. Execution is integral to strategy. People think of execution as the tactical side of business. That is a big mistake. Tactics are central to execution, but execution is not tactics. Execution is fundamental to strategy and has to shape it. No worthwhile strategy can be planned without taking into account the organization's ability to execute it. If you are talking about the smaller specifics of getting things done, call it process implementation, or sweating the details, or whatever you want. Nevertheless, do not confuse execution with tactics.

We mentioned that most companies develop strategy based on "what" – growth, etc. Companies that execute successfully know that strategy should be based around execution. Execution is a systematic process of rigorously discussing **hows** and **whats**, questioning, tenaciously following through, and ensuring accountability. It includes making assumptions about the business environment, assessing an organization's capabilities, linking strategy to operations and the people who are going to implement a strategy, synchronizing those people and their various disciplines, and linking rewards to outcomes. It also includes mechanisms for changing assumptions as the environment changes and upgrading a company's capabilities to meet the challenges of an ambitious strategy.

In a fundamental sense, execution is a systematic way of exposing truth and acting upon it. Most companies do not face the raw facts very well. That is the reason many have missed the mark at successfully implementing AI and analytics programs.

The heart of execution lies in three core systems:

1. Systems of people
2. Systems of strategy
3. Systems of operations

Every organization uses these systems in one form or another. However, most organizations treat them as independent silos. This is a mistake – they are interconnected pieces of a larger system.

Typically, during quarterly review sessions, the CEO and his senior leadership team allot less than half a day each year to review their plans – people, strategy, and operations.

People perform them mechanically, and as quickly as possible. They have real work they need to get back to and the review sessions are typically a bore – except for each leader's own presentation where they typically show the "best picture possible" rather than the most realistic one. Typically, the reviews are not particularly interactive. People sit passively watching PowerPoint presentations. They do not ask questions.

They do not debate, and as a result, they don't get much useful outcome. People leave with no commitments to the action plans they have helped create. This is a formula for failure. You need robust dialogue to surface the realities of the business. You need accountability for results – discussed openly and agreed to by those responsible – to get things done and reward the best performers. You need follow-through to ensure the plans are on track.

## CONSENSUS DECISIONS DO NOT EQUATE TO INTELLIGENT DECISION-MAKING – YOU *NEED* DEBATE!

"There is no correlation between consensus decisions and intelligent decisions. In the history of corporate history, most great decisions are made when there is still substantial disagreement in the air". – Jim Collins

And great decisions are taken without a need for consensus. The culture is one of disagreement, dialogue, debate, argument, pounding on tables, whatever, which leads to a point of clarity and, then in a corporate setting, is followed by executive decision and then cemented by a unified commitment behind it. That's the pattern that tends to correlate with better results.

The open, candid discussion, followed by planning and development of feedback mechanisms for these three systems, is where the things that matter about execution need to be decided. Businesses that execute perform them with rigor, intensity, and depth. They ask these incisive questions:

1. **Who will do the job? How will they be judged? How will they be held accountable?**
2. **What resources – human, technical, and financial resources are needed to execute the strategy?**
3. **Will the organization have the right resources two years out, when the strategy rises to the next level?**
4. **Can the strategy deliver the expected results or ROI?**
5. **How will success be measured?**
6. **Can it be broken down into achievable initiatives?**

People engaged in the process argue these questions, search out reality, and reach specific and practical conclusions. Everybody agrees about their responsibilities for getting things done, and everyone commits to those responsibilities. The systems are tightly linked with one another, not compartmentalized. Strategy takes account of people and operational realities. People are chosen and promoted in light of strategic and operational plans. Operations are linked to strategic goals and human capacities. Most important, the leader of the business and their leadership team are deeply engaged in all three. They are the **owners of the processes** – not the strategic planners or the human resources or finance.

### EXECUTION BREAKS DOWN IN FOUR WAYS – STEPHEN R. COVEY AND CHRIS MCCHESNEY

All organizations are composed of individuals, and unless you can get these individuals aligned to the organization's goals, you will not achieve these goals.

And the reason that most people don't achieve these goals is they don't define them.

Execution breaks down in four ways:

1. First, people in teams don't know the goals. Either there are too many goals or the goals are not clear.
2. Second, people and teams don't know what to do to achieve the goals. In other words, the goals are not translated in day-to-day activities.
3. Third, people and teams don't keep score. Few people can tell at any moment whether they are on track to achieve the goals that are important.
4. Fourth, people in teams don't account for results. People don't account to each other for progress on their most important goals.

While there is more technology and more choices than ever before, people have difficulty filtering through all of the competing priorities.

## *Job #1 for Leaders = Execution*

"Average people have great ideas. Legends have great execution". – Anonymous

Execution is the primary role of the leadership team. Many business leaders like to think that they are exempt from the details of actually running things. They can stand at the front of the ship – plotting the course and delegating the details to others. It is a pleasant way to view leadership. You are the strategist. You inspire your people with vision, while managers do the dirty work. This idea creates many aspirations for leadership, naturally. Who wouldn't want to have all the fun and glory while keeping their hands clean? This way of thinking is a fallacy, one that creates immense damage. Your AI and analytics program will only be successful if the leader's heart and soul believe in it and they are immersed in the details of implementing it within the company.

Leading is more than thinking big, or socializing with investors and other stakeholders. The leader has to be engaged personally and deeply in the business. Successful implementation of data-driven programs requires a comprehensive understanding of the business, its people, and its environment. The leader is the only person in a position to achieve that understanding. Only the leader can make execution happen, through their deep personal involvement in the substance and even the details of the program. Only a leader can ask the tough questions that everyone needs to answer, and then manage the process of debating the information and making the right trade-offs. Only the leader who is intimately engaged in the business can know enough to have the comprehensive view and ask the tough incisive questions.

## LEHMAN'S DICK FULD – MISTAKES AT THE HELM

The collapse of Lehman Brothers is a meaningful tale of a leadership misstep. CEO Dick Fuld successfully ran Lehman for years. Yet late in his tenure, he made some critical mistakes. When the financial crisis was brewing, he missed the significance of what was happening and instead of being turning inward and addressing the issues as a hands-on leader, he was out on business trips with clients, trying to grow the business. This was his Achilles heel, he was so often on a plane, so often trying to build the business and being bullish – he was not involved where he needed to be. Furthermore, he did something worse, he appointed a successor and delegated running the business to Joe Gregory. Joe was not up to the job – he was not sufficiently focused on the problems the company was facing. Some say that Dick tried to do the right thing and delegate, but in doing so he gave control to the wrong person.

Hiring the right people is the most important job a leader has to perform.

Only the leader can set the tone of the analytics dialogue in the organization. Dialogue is the core of culture and the basic unit of work. How people talk to each other absolutely determines how well the program will function. Is the dialogue stilted, politicized, fragmented, and butt-covering? Or, alternatively, is the dialogue candid and reality-based, raising the right questions, debating them, and finding realistic solutions? If it is the former – as it is in too many companies – reality will never come to the surface. If it is to be the latter, the leader has to be on the playing field with his or her management team, practicing it consistently and forcefully.

Leaders should not be micromanagers. Micromanaging is a big mistake. It diminishes people's self-confidence, saps their initiative, and stifles their ability to think for themselves. It's also a recipe for screwing things up – micromanagers rarely know as much about what needs to be done as the people that they're harassing, the ones who are dealing directly with the company's customers, and know what their customers actually need.

There's an enormous difference between leading an organization and presiding over it. The leader who boasts of a hands-off style or puts their faith in empowerment is not dealing with the issues. They are not confronting the people responsible for poor performance, or searching for problems to solve, and then making sure they get solved. If the company's leader is only presiding, they are only doing half of their job.

Leading for results is not about micromanaging, or being "hands on", or disempowering people. Rather, it's about active involvement – doing the things leaders should be doing in the first place. Leaders use their knowledge of the business to constantly probe and question. They bring weaknesses to light and rally their people to correct them.

The leader who gets results assembles an architecture responsible for results. They put in place a culture and processes for executing, and promoting people who get things done more quickly, including giving them greater rewards. Their personal involvement in the architecture is to assign the tasks and then follow up. This means making sure that people understand the priorities, which are based on his comprehensive understanding of the business, and asking incisive questions. The leader who delivers often does not even have to tell people what to do; they ask

> Leadership is an art form – there are different kinds of art – people have to find their own art.

questions so that people figure out what they need to do. In this way they coach them, passing on their experience as a leader in educating them to think in ways they never thought before. Far from stifling people, this kind of leadership helps them expand their own capabilities for leading.

A leader's interaction and communication needs to mean something. Boilerplate communication is worthless. What counts is the substance of the communication and the nature of the person doing the communicating – including their ability to listen as well as to talk.

Leaders who can do this are powerful and influential presences because they are the corporation. They are intimately and intensively involved with their people and operations. They connect because they know the realities and talk about them. They are knowledgeable about the details. They're excited about what they're doing. They're passionate about getting results. This is not "inspiration" through exhortation or speechmaking. These leaders energize everyone by the example they set with their "presence".

## Execution Must Be the DNA of the Organization's Culture

Execution must be enmeshed in every fiber of your organization. It has to be part of your organization's culture. It should be clear by now that execution isn't just another program you simply add onto your organization. A leader who says "okay, now we're going to execute an AI and analytics culture" is merely launching another fad of the

> "Organizational culture is the shared values, customs, traditions, rituals, behaviors, and beliefs shared in common by the members of that organization". – Anonymous

month. These programs are easily dismissed with no staying power. Just as the leader has to be personally involved in execution, so must everyone else in the organization understand and practice the discipline. It has to be a reflex, a habit.

It has to be embedded in the reward systems of the organization. Those who successfully execute will be positively rewarded. Those that cannot turn the corner will be retrained, moved to a different role in the organization, or helped to move on outside the organization. It must be a part of the normal behavior that all managers practice. Focusing on execution is not only an essential part of a business's culture, it is the one sure way to create meaningful cultural change.

## LESSONS FROM MAJOR LEAGUE BASEBALL – CONSEQUENCES OF MOVING PERSONNEL

There are multiple reasons for underperformance. It could be lack of knowledge or training. It could be mismatching someone with potential and placing them in the wrong job. It could be a temporary lapse caused by personal problems outside of work that will correct themselves in time. Or, it could be that the person is just not suited for success in your organization.

These are tough calls, but they must be made.

A very interesting study in human behavior was made by Hengchen Dai that moving someone into a new position can help those who have recently struggled, but erodes the motivation and execution of top performers (at least in major league baseball [MLB], but likely will translate to other organizations). The study was done with four decades of data by looking at batting averages among MLB players traded in mid-season. When players are traded across leagues, their batting statistics are reset – a fresh start. When they are traded within league, they keep their current statistics. Weak performers are given a second chance when traded across leagues. Strong performers lose their strong stats. The study used additional controls, but in the end – fresh starts often helped weak performers improve – they were motivated by the fresh start. However, the opposite occurred for strong performers – a reset appeared demotivating and often their performance went down.

Organizations are ripe with all sorts of performance measures that are constantly reset – monthly sales quotas, quarterly revenue reports, and annual personal review/bonus evaluation. Managers must be very careful and make nuanced approaches to framing performance fresh starts. Dai writes, "By recognizing that performance resets do not affect all individuals equally, organizations and managers can better harness the benefits and avoid the disadvantages of resets".

One way to think about execution is to think about it as the search for constant improvement. You take a critical look at the current state and you calibrate how far you are from your desired state and make corrections. The corrections you make are those you believe will get you to that desired state. Repeat. It's a relentless pursuit of reality; here you are, continually trying to find reality coupled with the processes for constant improvement. It is a huge change in behavior – a change in culture.

Leaders who execute look for gaps in managerial practices the same way. They move to close the gaps and raise the bar higher across the whole organization. The discipline of execution doesn't work unless everyone is on board and practicing it daily. It does not work if only a few people in the system practice it. Execution has to be part of the organization's culture driving the behavior of all leaders at all levels.

Execution must begin with senior leaders. It should cascade down to all executives. As Peter Drucker said, "an executive is anyone in an organization making decisions". In most organizations today, that is everyone. Each person needs to build and demonstrate their own skills. The results advance their careers, and they may just persuade others in the business to do the same. Thus, it becomes a corporate culture of execution.

## Why Don't People Get It?

If execution is so important, why is it so neglected? Organizations that are continuously executing are oblivious to it happening. It is like breath-

---
**Execution is like breathing.**

---

ing. You don't really notice it, it doesn't seem important, unless it stops. For organizations that are not executing, they know that something is missing when decisions aren't made or followed through and when commitments don't get met. They search and struggle for answers. They compare results to companies known to deliver on their commitments, looking for the answers in the organizational structure or processes or training. However, they rarely apprehend the underlying lesson, because execution hasn't yet been recognized or taught as a discipline. They literally don't know what they are looking for.

Execution is the stuff a leader delegates, right? That's the reason they have "people" so they can get involved in the details. Or, do great CEOs achieve their glory through execution? In fact, they do and there lies the great myth, the grand illusion. Leaders who believe they have arrived and no longer need the intellectual engagement with the organization suffer and the organization dies (see gray box, Leadership Failure – Hands-Off Leaders).

## LEADERSHIP FAILURE – HANDS-OFF LEADERS

Contrast great leaders versus the rest of the pack. Great leaders are hands-on in their management style. That does not mean they are micromanagers, they are just involved in the details of the business. Steve Jobs, Jack Welsh, Bill Gates, and Elon Musk are examples of leaders who could have played "king" and let others run their businesses in the later years, but remained involved and their businesses grew and flourished with their hands-on approach. So what is the difference between hands-on management versus hands-off management? Jean-Francois Manzoni defines the difference as shown in Table 2.1.

A hands-off management style will lead to failure in your analytics programs. A leader must be involved and

Table 2.1    Difference between a Hands-On Manager and a Hands-Off One

| Hands-On Manager | Hands-Off Manager |
|---|---|
| **Has a deep** understanding of the business with highly granular knowledge of the details | **Has limited** command of the details |
| **Wants to be kept** informed at a minimum, but will also interject ideas, suggestions, or even directions | **Does not make** much effort to get action plans from employees or insist on being kept up to speed |
| **Follows up** on agreed-upon actions to ensure expected outcomes | **Doesn't invest** much time in following up on agreements; employees are trusted to implement agreed-upon plans and to signal when they need help |

*Source:* Jean-Francois Manzonl, HBR.org

identify the organization's success factors. Then, by leadership working with the AI and analytics teams, together they translate these success factors into critical analytics capabilities. Then the AI and analytics team work through the data challenges and build the right technology to support these analytics capabilities.

Another example of hands-off leadership and arrogance is Dick Fuld, who led the largest financial disaster of our time – the failure of Lehman Brothers:

> His arrogant ego continuously grew, driven by his strong charismatic leadership, he not only refused to listen to any outside input but also didn't admit any mistake. His fatal conceit finally turned him into hopeless desperate. He lost the last chance to save Lehman Brothers and himself. His wrong intervention totally ruined the potential merger deal with Korea Development Bank. Euoo-Sung Min dislikes the assertive way that Fuld treated his buyer.
>
> … [H]is bad leadership also reflects on putting the wrong person in an important position. The worse example is COO, Joseph Gregory, who pushed Lehman employees to the brink by chasing new goals that ultimately doomed the firm. Nobody in Lehman Brothers likes Gregory except Fuld. Consequently, this wrong appointment cast a huge negative impact on the team.
>
> (Andrew Sorkin, *Too Big to Fail*)

This is a double failure – leaders have to be in the mix, leaders have to be in the details. Plus, leaders have to place the right people in the right positions – and if they make a mistake, they must make the tough choice to move them or let them go.

The fact is that great ideas most often come from the bottom of the organizations, not the top. People who are closest to the customer know better what the customer wants than the executive leadership team. This is a critical idea that must be incorporated in your AI and analytics program. The people in service or manufacturing operations know what the bottlenecks are and have ideas on how to improve efficiency. They are the idea generators. It is the executive team that needs to listen to these ideas, work with staff to crystalize them, bolster them, and evaluate the organization's capacity and budget required to implement them. Leaders need to get the right people and resources engaged, provide the structure to make sure there is a constant tracking of trajectory to target, correct where needed – to drive results – simply the ability to execute.

The leader's role is not as easy as it may sound. First, an atmosphere of trust and open dialogue has to be created. This is critical because if there is any mistrust, or people cannot be open and candid in their interchanges, things break down. All you get is nods and "uh hums" that go nowhere. Then, there is the intellectual challenge of execution which involves getting to the heart of an issue through persistent and constructive probing.

Suppose a manager presents a plan to make up a revenue gap in a quarterly review. The company has missed their numbers, but the manager assures leadership that they can make up the gap with an increase in sales over the next two quarters even though the market is flat. In their budget reviews, most leaders would accept a number without debate or discussion. However, in a results-based company's quarterly review, the leader will want to know if the goal is realistic. "Fine", the manager will say, "but where will the increase come from? What products will generate the growth? Who will buy them, and what pitch are we going to develop for those customers? What will our competitor's reaction be? What will our milestones be?"

If the leader has doubts about the organization's capacity to execute, they may drill down even further. "Are the right people in charge of getting it done", they may ask, "and is their accountability clear? Whose collaboration will be required, and how will they be motivated to collaborate? Will the reward system motivate them to a common objective?" In other words, the leader doesn't just sign off on a plan. They want an explanation, and they will drill down until the answers are clear. The leadership will elicit open conversation from others in the room. They will bring everyone's viewpoint out into the open. They will sense the reality of the situation and the degree of buy-in from this manager and others. The managers and people in the room have an opportunity to learn from this leader. In addition, the leader has an opportunity to learn from the people in the room. It's learning in real time. It is a way to make better decisions with accountability. If the room agrees to the plan, that manager is on the hook and not only accountable to the leader, but everyone present.

## THE DEFAULT LEADERSHIP
## POSITION SHOULD BE TRUST

Leadership is about trusting people, assuming they are going to do the right thing and at the same time knowing that people are flawed. They will disappoint at times. The default position should be trust.

There are multiple reasons for failure. One might be that a person is untrustworthy and they should not be trusted again. Another reason is incompetence. If this is the case, are they trainable? Can you help them get past their gaps? If you can, that employee often becomes the most loyal, most reliable employee you can have. A third reason for failure is a temporary lapse. People do have life events that perturb their performance. Does this person have an existing tack record? Is this failure the fluke, maybe it is a personal crisis? Regardless of which it might be, a leader will take the time, sit down, and have a deep and critical conversation to determine the reason for the failure and take appropriate action.

Organizations cannot succeed in today's competitive environment unless the right people, individually and collectively, focus on the right details at the right time. For you as a leader, moving from concept to the critical details to fruition is a long journey. You have to review a wide array of facts and ideas. You have to discuss what risks to take, and where to take them. You have to sort through these details selecting those that count. You have to assign them to the right people, and make sure these people align their work. Moreover, you have to make sure they are rewarded for their actions.

This decision-making requires intimate knowledge of the business and the external environment. It requires the ability to make accurate judgments about people. You have to accurately assess their capabilities, their reliability, their strengths, and their weaknesses. It requires commitment, focus, and incisive thinking. It requires superb skills in conducting candid, realistic dialogue.

# The Illusion of the Visionary Leader

> "True leadership isn't about having an idea. It's about having an idea and recruiting other people to execute on this vision". – Leila Janah

Great leaders do not become great because they have great ideas. Truly great leaders are great because they get things done – they seal the deal, plan and they execute.

Bill Gates was smart, but most of his ideas at Microsoft were not his own. What made him a great leader was he knew more than how to merely make speeches and rally the troops. He knew that he needed to ensure delivery – to be involved in the details. This does not mean he was a micromanager. However, it did mean that he could not simply delegate on high.

The product innovation details that separated Apple from the crowd did not originate with Steve Jobs! Many of the early advancements that Jobs adopted for the Mac were borrowed from other companies. What Jobs did was to tenaciously pursue the reality of the Mac – he made it come true, it happened. He "willed" it to be. He drove people to execute his plan. He was involved, he was relentless.

This is a great story on the power of execution. Xerox had the great ideas, yet they did not drive them into the hands of consumers. Steve Jobs did. Bill Gates did. Again – they were great leaders because they got things done – they set the plan and they executed.

This ability does not merely come from being tenacious or demanding. No, tyrants and bullies do not become great leaders. They may be successful for short bursts and short periods of accomplishment, but they do not have staying power.

**Here** is the *crux*: the magic skill set enables a leader to be able to break a broad vision into defined, specific, executable tasks. This leader is able to follow through on those tasks by insight, active engagement, and incisive communication. This leader has the ability to see ahead and discover any potential roadblocks as far as one is humanly possible. Moreover, when that is not possible, this leader has the ability to adapt quickly and correct for them.

This is not done in isolation – so another critical quality of a great leader is being able to pick the right people (for them to work with, with their style) to drive results forward. Great leaders know they cannot go it alone, they have to build out the right team – and not a team for the short term – not the use-them-up-and-spit-them-out mentality. But rather build and nurture a team that is built to last.

### THE TROUBLE WITH SAM – TWO-FACED SAM – SHORT GAME ONLY!

In corporate meetings, Sam, a senior VP of technology, was affable, well-liked, and funny – these meetings were great – 500 Zoom attendees were thinking: "What a great guy". That was a facade. The story was very different in his own organization – he was a tyrant, controlling, and extremely unreasonable. "I don't care about the details!" he was known to say in small meetings of his direct reports. "I just want people to get it done!!" He was not a team player or a team leader. He threatened people until he got his way or moved on.

Great leaders know that delivery of bad news offers moments for connecting and learning with employees. Getting to the heart of why things went wrong offers a leader a teaching moment for the employee and often a learning moment for the leader as well. It also establishes rapport and commitment to the relationship. This is the long game. This was not Sam.

What is the result of such actions – the best people leave! A 20+ year veteran who was loved by her colleagues could not stand it any longer – she left taking all her knowledge with her.

A new hire with less than a year under his belt was overwhelmed. Being called on a vacation day with his wife – Christmas eve shopping called back to his desk to correct someone else's work who Sam could not reach, so he called this poor surrogate to fill in. Bah Humbug!

**There were others that left due to Sam's toxic nature.**

He would also talk about his employees with his reports – "We will name and shame!" That was one of Sam's games. This may work in the short run, making people feel guilty for leadership's aggression, but it cripples the long game. These leaders have records of a two-year average, some may last four years if they can convince, the good ole boys and gals they are worth keeping around – they are not! Sam had a two- and three-year tenure across the companies he worked.

Sam was not involved in details; he did not want to be involved in the details. His game was the short game, come in and intimidate – that would move the needle a year or so and that was all he needed. Sam (and leaders like him) only need two to three years at a company; that was Sam's record. He only needed to come in, carpet bomb, claim victory, move on to a higher salary – a very effective short game.

# Leadership Priorities for Establishing Successful AI and Analytics Programs

In this section, we focus on **personal behaviors** a leader must embody to create and implement a successful AI and analytics program.

## *Understand Your People and Your Business*

Leaders have to live and breathe their businesses. You cannot initiate or carry forward a successful analytics program if you reign on high. Companies that don't execute successful programs often have leaders who are out of touch with the day-to-day realities. They're getting lots of information delivered to them, but it's filtered – it is what they want to hear or presented by direct reports and their own perceptions, limitations, and agendas. True leaders are where the action is. They are getting information firsthand. They are not getting it secondhand. They are engaged with the business, so they know their organizations comprehensively. More importantly, they know their people. Not necessarily on a personal level (although that is good), but how to read them so they can understand the reality.

They are willing to understand what their leaders are struggling with and are committed to finding out how a data-driven experience can provide success for everyone. They know the business, they know the people, they understand that a change has to happen, and that change involves a data-driven shift of problem-solving and action.

### LEADERSHIP INVOLVEMENT IS MORE THAN SMALL TALK

Just because a leader visits a plant and asks about how people's kids are doing or about the World Series, that doesn't mean they're an involved leader. Management by walking around (MBWA, Circa Tom Peters) does not mean anything if you don't get to the heart of the business. It's like politicians that go to Iraq or Afghanistan and visit the troops without really talking to leadership about what's happening on the ground. They come back and make speeches and talk about progress, although they really know nothing about what's actually happening in the military theater. The military leaders may watch the media present this and feel frustrated that the highest leadership doesn't really care about what is going on. The same can be true for business. Good leaders are engaged with the business and want to be asked incisive difficult questions by the senior leadership. They want to be engaged. They want to be questioned as it clarifies their thoughts. They want validation that the aims they're taking are agreed upon with the senior leaders.

## Eliminate the Inside Game: Insist on Facts

There are two things that can inhibit candid and open communication. These behaviors greatly limit the level of success you can achieve and therefore have to be overcome. First, organizations are full of office politics and personal agendas, and this creates false narratives. Second, people will omit important information in exchanges. They avoid realism and hide mistakes. They either want to be kind or they want to avoid being uncomfortable presenting the complete story.

How do you create an environment for open and candid exchanges? **First**, if leaders know their people and their people trust them, they can then insist on the facts. There is no way to get at the truth if everyone is guarded or does not trust your leadership – and they need to trust all leadership. You can then start to establish transparent, clear, open exchanges.

**Second**, leaders need to model the same behavior they want to see. They have to not hide their shortcomings or failures. They can't sugarcoat their strikeouts and play power trips. They have to model the importance of being honest and forthcoming even when it is uncomfortable. They should focus on strengths, but candidly admit their weaknesses.

**Third**, leaders must eliminate people's fear of telling the truth. We have all heard, "don't shoot the messenger". There is good reason it is popular – it is true. The quickest way to get people to close up is to shut them down, scold them, or not listen to them when they present bad news (see gray box, The Trouble with Sam – We Call Him RADIO Sam).

### REALISM AND THE TRUTH – THE NEED TO MATCH AI AND ANALYTICS CAPABILITY INTERNALLY AND EXTERNALLY

We will be talking about assessment and planning in a later section. However, it is important to note that you need accurate assessments (accuracy, realism, and the truth) both externally and internally of your AI and analytics capability. You then need to match the analytics execution to the intersection of both.

Externally, what is the market doing? What are the forces that are acting upon the market today and how will they shift tomorrow?

Internally, what capabilities do we have or could acquire to meet these challenges? How can we improve with AI and analytics – what secret sauce can we create?

## Goal Setting

We are about to dive into goal setting. First, we need to make an important distinction about the nature of goals and how they are related to lead and lag measures.

## A CRITICAL NOTE ON GOALS –
## LEAD AND LAG MEASURES

How we measure our progress toward goals is critical. Great measures are just as important or more important than the goals themselves, because they track our activities applied to the goals. When working toward a goal, we should measure our success by activities that are highly correlated, or better yet, causative to the outcome – our goal. We do not act upon the goal itself. We act on the correlative activities. These correlative activities happen before we attain the outcome. We track them with lead measures.

A simple example might be beneficial. Take weight loss.

If we want to lose weight. We should not focus too much on the scale. Weight loss is a lag measure, our goal. Lag measures are often the goal.

If you just focus on weighing in every morning, you will likely be disappointed. However, we know that diet is highly correlated with weight loss. We also know it precedes the weight on the scale. The amount of activity or exercise is also correlative and precedes the weight on the scale. We should focus on diet and exercise to attain our goal of losing 10 pounds.

However, we do not operate on the lag measure directly. Losing weight requires a set of disciplines and these disciplines influence our outcome and help us reach our goal. We chart our progress with these "lead" measures. To lose weight, we chart our progress of adhering to a diet, physical exercise, general physical activity, and sleep. Acting on these lead activities and measuring progress should influence our goal. If we are consistent in measuring and achieving our goals on these lead measures (and we have the right lead measures), our objective will be attained.

To track our success, we need to distinguish measures that track the goals and measures that track our progress toward the goal. Goals are the end game and they can be messy. There are many things that might influence weight. However, there are only a few that we can directly control. Those are the things we must work on as measures to track our progress. If for some reason the goal is not coming in time (there will be a lag), then we must reassess. Are there things we can influence and are there things important that we are not acting upon? Is there a one time, external factor that dominated the outcome over and above our efforts.

**Important caveat #1:** We must have the **right lead measures**. These measures must be predictive, meaning if we perform those activities, they will affect our objective. In our losing weight example, it has been well documented that diet and exercise influence weight loss. There is also new research showing that sleep and general activity have an effect as well.

**Important caveat #2:** We must be able to **influence these lead measures**. If we have no control over the measures, then they cannot serve us. In our losing weight scenario, it is well known that genetics effect our ability to lose weight, but since we have no control over our genetics (at least not yet), this is not a good measure to concentrate on efforts.

Reference: Stephen Covey and Chris McChesney, *The 4 Disciplines of Execution®* (2007).

## *Set the Minimum Number of Goals Possible and Make Them Crystal Clear*

If you have great management and staff in your organization, they are very busy, they are working hard to support daily tasks and operational duties. They are adapting to a changing environment. They are responding to the "now" of the tactical business landscape. They have full calendars, full days, and full weeks to support the existing business and operations. Now, on top of that, you are launching new initiatives. You want to add an AI and analytics program so that you can survive in the changing world of digital transformation.

What is the natural consequence when you want people to undergo training and sit in planning sessions for a new program initiative? They sit in meetings and they think, "this is great, but I need to get back to my day job", or they do not attend, citing a crisis they have to fix immediately. One reason for this is that there are too many goals, but they are *not* clear (more on that in the next section).

The natural reaction may be to push back or at least make these initiatives secondary to their existing "full plate" of "real work".

The leader who says "I've got 10 priorities" doesn't know what they're talking about – they don't know themselves – they don't know what the most important things are. You have to have a few vital, clearly realistic goals and priorities, which will influence the overall performance of the company.

Leaders who execute well focus on very few clear priorities that everyone can grasp. Why just a few? First, anybody who thinks through the logic of a business will see that focusing on three or four priorities will produce the best results from the resources at hand. Second, people in contemporary organizations need a small number of clear priorities to execute well. In an old-fashioned hierarchical company, this wasn't so much of a problem – people generally knew what to do, because the orders came down through the chain

> "The difference between successful people and really successful people is that really successful people say 'no' to almost everything". – Warren Buffett

of command. But when decision-making is decentralized or highly fragmented, as in a matrix organization, people at many levels have to make endless trade-offs. There is competition for resources and ambiguity over decision rights and working relationships. Without carefully thought-out and clear priorities, people can get bogged down in warfare over who gets what and why.

Along with having clear goals, you should strive for simplicity. One thing you will notice about leaders who get things accomplished is that they speak simply and directly. They talk plainly and forthrightly about what is on their mind. They know how to simplify things so that others can understand them, evaluate them, and act on them, so what they say becomes common sense. Sometimes it takes a new pair of eyes to clarify priorities – see gray box on how Steve Jobs came back to Apple with a new set of eyes.

> "Wise men speak because they have something to say; Fools because they have to say something". – Plato

## A LESSON IN FOCUS AND LESS IS MORE – STEVE JOBS

When Steve Jobs returned to Apple in 1997, the tech company he cofounded more than two decades earlier was on the brink of failure. One of the first efforts undertaken by Jobs was to reorient the company, to provide laser focus. The product line had exploded and Apple was producing multiple versions of the same product to satisfy requests from retailers

When Jobs asked product managers why so many products were necessary, they did not have an answer, so Jobs asked another question, "Which ones do I tell my friends to buy?" When he didn't get a simple answer, he reduced the number of Apple products by 70%.

Jobs says in his biography: "Deciding what not to do is as important as deciding what to do. It's true for companies, and it's true for products". Moving forward, Jobs' strategy was to produce only four products. The move to a smaller product line and a greater focus on quality and innovation paid off. We know the rest of the story.

More is not better. Focus is.

Reference: *Steve Jobs: The Exclusive Biography.*

## Target Goals and Make Them Operational

Goals and objectives have to be specifically targeted for the level and function of the organization. They start at the corporate level, in the C-suite, and then they cascade across and down the organization. AI and analytics C-suite objectives may look something like:

1. Applying data-driven analytic technologies, we will reduce customer attrition 10% in the coming year and 20% in the two subsequent years by targeting at risk customers and initiating "next best actions" based on machine learning models and visual analytics.
2. Applying data-driven analytic technologies, we will reduce new customer acquisition cost by 20% per customer in the coming year and 30% in the two subsequent years by more intelligently targeting customers.
3. Applying data-driven analytic technologies, we will improve median margin rates per product by 2% in the coming year and 3.5% in the two subsequent years by more intelligently segmenting customers and employing price optimization algorithms per segment.

**Note**: The fewer goals the better. You want to be very targeted and specific and should only have one to three goals. More AI and analytics idea/project generation is provided in our *It's All Analytics: Part III* book that links business initiatives to AI and analytics capabilities. In addition, see the chapter "Anatomy of a Business Decision" in our *It's All Analytics – Part II: Designing an Integrated AI, Analytics, and Data Science Architecture for Your Organization.*

Each member of the C-suite then takes each of these goals and determines how they will support them. They will write one to three goals specific to their unit that align with the corporate goal. Then each director will do the same for their division and each manager for their department. Goals at the department level will be very specific and targeted along with tactics on how to achieve them. Each level has one to three goals that contribute to the achievement of the C-suite goals.

An important note is that goals at the corporate level do not vary much within the planning (yearly) cycle. However, as you move down the levels within the organization, the goals often must change due to the external market conditions and internal factors.

The natural reaction may be to push back or at least make these initiatives secondary to their existing "full plate" of "real work".

## Make Goals Personal

At the staff level, goals should be personal and targeted. Staff members should mutually sign off on agreed-upon goals that align with the department goals. Managers should do the same with directors and on up.

Why is this so important? Most times, these AI and analytic goals are outside the normal day-to-day requirements and activities. When things are urgent, what is the focus? The day job, i.e., the normal day-to-day activities. Therefore, there needs to be a minimum number of these goals, these goals must be focused, and each team member must contribute in their own way with their unique skill set. They must be "personal" according to ability and contribution. They must also be "personal" in reward.

## A SIMPLE FORMULA FOR GOAL SETTING AND ATTAINMENT – X TO Y BY *WHEN*

A very simple formula that captures the essence of achieving goals is X to Y by when. X is the current state, Y is the desired, future state. You need to be specific and realistic. Specify X, the current state, where you are presently. Specify Y, the future state you want to get to. Then consider the resources it will take to move from X to Y. Consider how long it will take to get there. That is the *When.*

## *Make Goals Measurable*

We touched on this previously when we spoke to lead and lag measures. Our goal is often a lead measure, it is what we want in the end, but it is not something we can directly act upon. We act upon lead measures. Lead measures are predictive and influenceable. We gave the example of the lag measure being the goal to lose weight. Two

"Perhaps what you measure is what you get. More likely, what you measure is all you'll get. What you don't (or can't) measure is lost". – H. Thomas Johnson

lead measures were diet and activity; they are predictive and influenceable.

However, beyond these requirements, we have to be able to get at these measures. They have to be available within our current data systems or we have to be committed to making them available. We will measure both lead and lag measures, paying particular attention to our lead measures, tracking our progress.

As Peter Drucker said, you cannot manage what you cannot measure. Measurement is critical.

## Follow Through

Clear, simple goals will not mean much if nobody takes them seriously. The failure to follow through is widespread in business, and is a major cause of poor execution. How many meetings have you attended where people left without firm conclusions about who should do what and when? Everybody may have agreed the idea was good, but since nobody was named accountable for the results, it doesn't get done.

What are the specifics? Who will lead the effort, i.e., be accountable for the results? Who will support them in this effort? When are results expected? Does this group have any authority to act upon the results or make them operational? Will you need budget? If so, is there budget available or will you have to wait until the next budget cycle? Are the results time sensitive? **It is so easy to say that is a good idea – follow-through is hard!**

Follow through should be rewarded. You want doers in your analytics programs, not merely theorists or big talkers. You do not want perfectionists. You want people who can drive to results and when you find these people, you need to reward them so everyone sees what is important.

## Reward Program Performers

If you want people to produce specific results, you reward them accordingly. This fact seems so obvious that it shouldn't need saying. Yet many corporations do such a poor job of linking rewards to performance that there's little correlation at all. They don't distinguish between those who achieve results and those who don't.

Furthermore, you need to set up a separate reward system for your AI and analytics program – this must be separate from regular work. As we have said, in the next few coming years – companies that do not implement successful AI and analytics programs will not survive, period. You should set up a different pool of bonuses that are directly tied to the employee's contribution to the AI and analytics program. You should set targets at the beginning of each quarter with specific goals and the monetary figure you are offering if the employee meets their targets. You must be critical in your assessment and reward strong performers over 100% and underperformers much less than 100%.

Your managers cannot accept "well, I didn't contribute much to the AI and analytics program because I was busy with urgent matters" as an excuse to reward employees out of the analytics bonus pool. Yes, these employees should be compensated in other ways. That is why it is critical to separate your bonus programs. With time, if you fund the analytics bonus program sufficiently, it will incentivize people into the behavior you want to see and what is needed to make your program successful.

## Expand People's Capabilities

In the previous paragraph, we covered an example of an employee that did not understand why they were not receiving an AI and analytics program bonus, since they "had to spend all their time" on operational activities and urgent matters. Obviously, this could lead to frustration of some employees and even losing some good people. How do you circumvent this? **Be an active coach**. Coaching is the single most important part of expanding others' capabilities. Coaching builds awareness. Coaching empowers choice and leads to change. It's the difference between giving orders and teaching people how to get things done. Good leaders regard every encounter as an opportunity to coach.

As a leader, you've acquired a lot of knowledge and experience – even wisdom – along the way. One of the most important parts of your job is passing it on to the next generation of leaders. This is how you expand the capabilities of everyone else in the organization, individually and collectively.

The most effective way to coach is to observe a person in action and then provide specific useful feedback. The feedback should point out examples of behavior and performance that are good or that need to be changed. One example of an opportunity to coach and provide feedback is in the quarterly AI and analytics program reviews.

Another opportunity is in meetings. When the leader discusses business and organizational issues in a group setting, everyone learns. Wrestling with challenging issues collectively, exploring pros and cons and alternatives, and deciding which one makes sense increase people's capabilities, both individually and collectively – if it's done with honesty and trust.

The skill of the coach is the art of questioning. Asking incisive questions forces people to think, to discover, to search.

## A Leader's Character

A leader not only knows their own strengths and weaknesses, they are able to make the tough calls when it counts. Leadership requires strength of character, it is critical. Leaders that are successful in analytics execution have emotional strength, can be honest with themselves, deal honestly with business and organizational realities, and give people straightforward, direct assessments.

You must accept the diversity of viewpoints, values, and personal backgrounds that enrich your organization. You must learn to listen, make hard decisions, and communicate those decisions. You must adapt internally to the team, you have to know when to listen and give in when it makes sense, and draw the line when it doesn't. Externally, you must accept the challenge of a constantly changing business environment and be strong enough to quickly adapt to it. If you can't do these things, your AI and analytics program will not succeed.

As a leader, it takes emotional strength to accept whatever information you receive and not react and kill the messenger. The tyrant or irate leader will only alienate their people and the information they get will be filtered to whatever the messenger thinks they want to hear – rather than the raw, objective truth.

Moreover, if a leader is going to be able to adapt and steer the analytics program in the right direction and if they are going to learn what is working and what is failing in the program, they need the right information. A scientist or an engineer cannot do their jobs with bad data. A leader will do the same with the wrong information. It is that simple. This information is critical in running the enterprise and making corrections. Emotional strength gives you the courage to accept points of view that are the opposite of yours and deal with conflict, and the confidence to not only accept challenges in meetings, but to encourage them. It enables you to accept and deal with your own weaknesses, be firm with people who are not performing, and handle the ambiguity inherent in a fast-moving, complex organization.

Emotional strength comes from self-discovery and self-mastery. It is the foundation of people skills. Good leaders learn their specific personal strengths and weaknesses, especially in dealing with other people, and then build on the strengths and correct the weaknesses. They earn their leadership when the followers see their inner strength, inner confidence, and ability to help team members deliver results, while at the same time expanding their own capabilities.

A solid, long-term leader has an ethical frame of reference that gives them the power and energy to carry out even the most difficult assignment. They never waver from what they think is right. This characteristic is beyond honesty or beyond integrity, beyond treating people with dignity. It is a business leadership ethic.

Leaders in modern organizations may be able to get away with emotional weaknesses for a time, but they cannot hide them for long. They face challenges to their emotional strength all the time. Failure to meet these challenges gets in the way of achieving results. Getting things done depends ultimately on performing a specific set of behaviors. Without emotional strength, it is tough to develop these behaviors either in ourselves or in others. How can your organization face reality if people do not speak honestly, and if its leaders do not have the confidence to surface and resolve conflicts or give and take honest criticism? How can a team correct mistakes or improve if its members don't have the emotional strength to admit they don't have all the answers?

Putting the right people in the right job requires emotional strength. Failure is usually the result of leaders with emotional weakness. Without emotional strength, you will have a hard time hiring the best people to work for you. Because if you are lucky, these "best new hires" will be better than you are; they will bring new ideas and energy to your operation. A manager who is emotionally weak will avoid such people out of their fear they will undercut his power. Their tendency will be to protect their fragile authority. They will surround themselves with people they can count on to be loyal and exclude those who will challenge them with new thinking. Eventually, such emotional weaknesses will destroy both the leader and the organization.

Another emotional weakness leads to not making touch decisions of what to do with problem employees. **Failure to deal with underperformers is an extremely common**

**problem in corporations**. We discuss this further in the section "A Key Driver of Changing Behavior".

**Four core qualities make up emotional strength:**

**Authenticity**: People have an uncanny way of sniffing out a fake. You might be able to fool people for a short time, but it won't take long to determine if your character is authentic. Your outer person is the same as your inner person, not a mask you put on. Who you are is the same as what you do and say. Only authenticity builds trust, because eventually people spot the fakers.

Whatever leadership ethics you may preach, people will watch what you do. If you are cutting corners, even the best people will lose faith in you. The worst will follow your example. The rest will do what they must do to survive in a muddy ethical environment. This becomes a pervasive barrier to getting things done.

**Self-Awareness Coupled with Self-Acceptance**: Self-awareness is the core of authenticity. When you know yourself and you are comfortable with your strengths and not crippled by your shortcomings, you can be authentic. You know your behavioral blindsides in emotional blockages, and you have a modus operandi for dealing with them – you draw on the people around you. Self-awareness gives you the capacity to learn from your mistakes as well as your successes. It enables you to keep growing.

Nowhere is self-awareness more important than in a performance culture, which taps every part of the brain and emotional makeup. Few leaders have the intellectual acumen to do it all. To do it all, a leader must be a good judge of people, a good strategist, and provide good operational management, while at the same time being available to customers and doing a myriad of other things the job demands. It can be too much. However, if you know where you are lacking, at least you can reinforce those areas and get some help from your leadership team or business unit. You can put mechanisms in place to help you get it done. The person who does not even recognize where they are lacking never gets it done.

**Self-Mastery**: When you know yourself, you can master yourself. You can keep your ego in check, take responsibility for your behavior, adapt to change, embrace new ideas, and adhere to your standards of integrity and honesty under all conditions.

Self-mastery is the key to true self-confidence. We are talking about the kind that is authentic and positive, as opposed to the kinds that mask weakness or insecurity – the studied demeanor of confidence, or outright arrogance.

Self-confident people contribute the most to meaningful conversations. Their inner security gives them a methodology for dealing with the unknown and for linking it to the actions that need to be undertaken. They know that they don't know everything; they are actively curious, and encourage debate to bring up opposite views and set up the cultural atmosphere of learning from others. They can take risks, and relish hiring people who are smarter than they are. So when they encounter a problem, they don't have to whine, cast blame, or feel like victims. They know they'll be able to fix it.

**Humility**: The more you can contain your ego, the more realistic you are about your problems. You learn how to listen and admit that you don't know all the answers. You exhibit the attitude that you can learn from anyone at any time. Your pride doesn't get in the way of gathering the information you need to achieve the best results.

It doesn't keep you from sharing the credit that needs to be shared. Humility allows you to acknowledge your mistakes. Making mistakes is inevitable, but good leaders both admit and learn from them and over time create a decision-making process based on experience.

How do you develop these qualities in yourself? There are, of course, books on the subject; some of them useful. But the ultimate learning comes from paying attention to experience. As people reflect on their experiences, or as they get coached, blockages crumble and emotional strengths develop. Sometimes the insights come from watching others' behavior; your observational capabilities make you realize that you have a blockage that you need to correct. Either way, as you gain experience in self-assessment, your insights lead to self-improvement that expands your personal capacity.

Such learning is not an intellectual exercise. It requires tenacity, persistence, and daily engagement. It requires reflection and modifying personal behavior. The behavior of a business's leader is, ultimately, the behavior of the organization. As such, it is the foundation of the culture.

## SEVEN BELIEFS AND BEHAVIORS THAT GROWTH LEADERS EXHIBIT

We have covered many qualities needed to be an effective leader in this section. McKinsey (Biljana Cvetanovski, Eric Hazan, Jesko Perrey, and Dennis Spillecke, September 2019) provide "Seven Beliefs and Behaviors that Growth Leaders Share". We note these seven points and then take liberty to apply them more specifically to your AI and analytics program success.

1. **I am all in**. We have covered this previously. Successful leaders are hands-on in the details of developing the strategy and aligning the organization to that strategy.
2. **I am willing to fail**. Organizations that do not embrace and implement viable AI and analytics programs will surely fail. Leaders must be willing to take on the challenge.
3. **I know my customer as a person**. We believe all business is about serving customers and we believe in a broader view of customer in the way Edward R. Deming did – anyone who is receiving the product of your work, whether they are internal or external to the organization, is a customer. The only way to fulfill their needs is to know them well and that requires deep communication – and we believe knowing your customer qualitatively and quantitatively helps understand them.
4. **I favor action over perfection**. Iterating quickly and converging to great over time is much better than trying to get it perfect the first time. You will learn with each analytics project, so the best way to improve is to garner quick, iterative gains.
5. **I fight for growth**. We translate that in our case as I fight for data-driven decision-making. Even the most incisive leaders can always validate their positions with analytics.
6. **I have a growth story I tell all the time**. We translate this to the appropriate analytics story – one appropriate for the audience. We continually tell success stories about better decisions and actions based on data. Data-driven storytelling is becoming quite popular and is part of data literacy that we discuss in the last section.
7. **I give control to others**. Leaders must use the collective intelligence of the entire organization. We have covered this in multiple sections.

# Foundations of the New AI and Analytics Culture

There is a lot of lip service paid to "culture", but there are not many leaders investing time and money into practical solutions that influence data-driven cultures. It is mostly platitudes and speeches. Proof point – Tom Davenport stated in a 2020 interview for a Harvard Business webinar that trillions of dollars are spent around the globe in data infrastructure each year and he estimated that about US$ 1 trillion per year is spent on analytics every year. Then he stated, **"How much is spent on data oriented cultures? Not very much!"**

Why is this? **First**, people love sexy stuff and technology that supports data, AI and analytics is sexy. People issues, developing culture, this softer stuff isn't sexy. **Second**, it is more difficult to determine cultural gaps and change the direction of a culture. Computers do what they are programmed to do – you cannot program people. People often respond in ways that are difficult to understand.

Culture Eats Strategy for Breakfast

People's beliefs and behaviors are the heart of culture.

> To succeed in your AI and analytics programs – *you have to create the proper culture.*

An innovative culture is centered on data. For most organizations, this means changing the current culture.

> While leaders love to talk strategy – *Culture Eats Strategy for Breakfast.*

Most efforts at cultural change fail because they are not linked to improving business outcomes. The ideas and tools of cultural change are fuzzy and disconnected from strategic and operational realities. To change a company culture, you need a set of processes that will change the beliefs and behaviors of people in ways that are directly linked to the bottom-line results.

The basic premise is simple. Cultural change happens when your aim is to accomplish key results and perform at new levels. You do not need complex theory, focus groups, or employee surveys to use this framework. You need to change people's behavior so that they produce results. First, you tell people clearly what results you are looking for. Then you discuss how to get those results, as a key element of the coaching process. Then you reward people for producing the results. If they came up short, you provide additional coaching, withdraw rewards, give them other jobs, or let them go. This may sound harsh, but you and all parties are better off by separating and moving on when necessary. When you do these things, you create a culture of getting things done.

## *Making Culture Work*

There is a saying that is often repeated: "we do not think ourselves into a new way of acting; we act ourselves into a new way of thinking". This is often repeated because it is true.

The heart of an organization's culture is its actions, practices, its accepted conventions. and standards. It is the sum of its shared values, beliefs, and norms of behavior. People who are setting out to change the culture often talk about changing the set of values. That is the wrong approach. Values, fundamental principles, and standards, such as integrity or respect for the customer, may need to be reinforced, but they rarely need changing.

The beliefs that influence specific behaviors are more likely to need changing. These beliefs are conditioned by training, experience, what people hear inside or outside about the company's prospects, and perceptions about what leaders are doing and saying. People change them only when new evidence shows persuasively that they are false. For example, if people in an organization believe they are in a mature industry with no growth prospects, they won't spend a lot of time and energy intensively looking for growth opportunities. They believe others who do less than they do will get the same rewards; however, that belief will drain their energy and prevent them from finding the reality of their company's situation.

## EXECUTION MAKES ALL THE DIFFERENCE IN THE WORLD

In a senior leadership meeting, a CEO asked the team members to identify the most critical beliefs that had shaped the company's view of itself in the past five years, and also the beliefs most needed now for the journey forward. Working in groups, they came up with the following lists.

### OLD BELIEFS

*We are in a commodity business.* We are in a slow growth, mature industry – lots of competitors, little differentiation, and that means inherently low profit margins.

*We can't grow at market rates.* We are the biggest player in a commodity business. We have difficulty finding profitable growth.

*Profits follow revenues.* Only if we grow, can we get more profit.

*Each leader owns all resources – control is key.* Each division has total autonomy and safeguards its turf.

*My peer is my competitor.* We are in a zero sum game.

*People aren't accountable.* It isn't my fault.

*We know more than our clients do.* Our people will tell the client what solution they need.

**NEW BELIEFS**

*We can grow faster than the market – profitability, and using capital efficiently.*

*We can increase productivity year in and year out.*

*We are committed to our clients' success.*

*We will achieve service excellence.*

*Collaboration is the key to our success.*

*We are going to be accountable and committed.*

*We will be better listeners to our clients.*

The second list became the agenda for the attitude change, not only among top executives, but among all leaders within the organization.

Behaviors are beliefs turned into action. Behaviors deliver the results. They are where the rubber meets the road. When we talk about behavior, we are talking less about individual behavior than about norms of behavior: the accepted, expected ways groups of people behave in the corporate setting – the "rules of engagement" as some people call them. The norms are about how people work together. As such they are critical to a company's ability to create a competitive advantage.

## A Key Driver of Changing Behavior

Some say, "it may go without saying" and/or "of course that is what we are all about"; but sometimes what is obvious is not practiced. To change behavior you have to change practices, and to change practices you have to have the right incentives in place. If there is no incentive to change, change will not happen.

In moving to a data-driven culture, making AI and analytics the embodiment of our organization will take commitment, planning, and money. It may not take more of any of those

three; however, it will take a realignment of all three. You
need leadership and management to commit to a new way of
thinking and the dedication and patience to see it through.
You need to carefully consider your specific organization,
industry, and design a new plan – the way your business will
succeed with AI. You then need to push the commitment and
plan down the ranks. To do this, you need to incentivize the
ranks. What is in it for them? Change is hard and unless the
gain is better than the pain, no one will change.

A business's culture reflects what is appreciated and
respected. Ultimately, it reflects what gets rewarded. It tells
the people in the organization what is valued and recognized,
and in the interest of trying to make their own careers more
successful, that is where they will concentrate. If a company
rewards and promote people for effecting data-driven change
and analytics promotion, its culture will change. Far too many
companies do a poor job of linking rewards to performance.

**What's the problem?**

Leaders and managers often behave like wimps. They talk
about making the hard choices, about separating the winners
and losers in performance reviews. Then when it comes time
to act, they compress everyone to right around the middle
of the pack and thus people do not see the contrast of high
performers to middling performers to underperformers. They
will hear excuses about why people are not taking initiative and engaging in analytics changes – or even attending
analytics education – "I have a day job, I have to get the TPS
report prepared". The manager agrees and does not fight back
against this – then people don't change, they don't promote
analytics, and they end up doing the same job. When people
don't change, the ways of business stay the same.

We will say it again:

> *Organizations that cannot succeed with analytics will
> die.*

Your organization cannot succeed with analytics until you have a data-driven culture. Your organization cannot succeed unless you tie rewards to the cultural change.

However, people have issues making the tough calls and sticking with them. They don't have the emotional strength to give straightforward, honest feedback. Poor leaders will not withhold a reward or penalize people for poor performance. They do not feel comfortable rewarding performance and behavior. They procrastinate, sugarcoat, and rationalize. Leaders sometimes even create new jobs for nonperformers. As a result, the culture is damaged, performance is hampered, and results suffer.

## Social Operating Mechanisms (SOMs)

### SOCIAL OPERATING MECHANISMS

Ram Charan (consultant, author, and HBR contributor) introduced a concept called social operating mechanisms (SOMs) which are processes to motivate people at all levels and have them connected seamlessly as a team all the time.

Two things make SOMs extremely powerful. First, they are integrative, cutting across the organization and breaking (down) barriers among units, functions, disciplines, work processes, and hierarchies and between the organization and the external environment as well. SOMs create new information flows and new working relationships. They let people who normally don't have much contact with one another exchange views, share information and ideas, and learn to understand their company as a whole. They achieve transparency and simultaneous action.

Second, SOMs are where the beliefs and behaviors of the culture are practiced consistently and relentlessly. They help spread the leaders' beliefs, behaviors, and mode of dialogue throughout the organization.

Breaking a culture of indecision or inaction will require leaders to challenge assumptions, share information, and bring disagreement to the surface. Charan offers the following example to highlight the signs of indecision:

> How many meetings have you attended where everyone seemed to agree at the end about what actions would be taken but nothing much actually happened as a result?
>
> A presentation is made to a meeting about a proposed project. There is silence until the CEO speaks and asks questions that show they have taken a position on the matter and made up their mind. Then others speak up to agree with the CEO, keeping their comments positive.
>
> It appears that everyone supports the project. But, some are concerned and keeping their reservations to themselves. Over the next few months the project is slowly strangled to death.
>
> It is not clear who killed it but it is clear that the true sentiment in the room after the presentation was the opposite of the apparent consensus.

The key issue is that the true sentiment is the opposite of the apparent consensus. Charan says that "silent lies and lack of closure" can lead to a false decision that is undone by unspoken factors and inaction.

Charan has identified common factors in examples of indecision:

- A "misfire" in the personal interactions that are supposed to produce results. The people responsible for

reaching a decision and acting on it have failed to connect and engage with each other.

■ Intimidated by the group hierarchy and constrained
by formality and lack of trust, people go through the
motions without conviction or commitment.

■ Lacking emotional commitment, the people who must
implement the decision don't act decisively.

Leaders often create a culture of indecisiveness or inaction. The good news is that leaders can break through it
with their discourse and interactions. They should challenge assumptions, share critical information, and bring
disagreement to the surface.

Some SOMs can be directly influenced by leadership. These
include organizational structure, design of rewards, compensation and sanctions, design of metrics, IT systems, communication systems, and hierarchical distribution of power, where
such things as assigned tasks and budget-level approvals are
visible, hardwired, and informal. Leadership has a great deal
of input and control over these SOMs.

The SOMs where leadership has only indirect control or
lesser control include the values, beliefs, and norms of behavior, along with everything else that isn't directly designed by
leadership or management. The major impact leaders have is
the behavior they demonstrate in their organizations and the
behavior they reward.

Structure divides an organization into units designed to
perform certain jobs. The design of structure is obviously
important, but it is the softer side of leadership that integrates
the organization into a unified, synchronized whole. Social
relationships, the norms of behavior, the power relationships,

flows of information, and flows of decisions – these are culture – and culture is king.

## Breaking Barriers and Improving SOMs – Two Organizational Structures

One of the most useful things leaders can do is to create an environment of collaboration and sharing – an environment of teamwork. One of the easiest parts of that is to break down traditional functional structures. One consideration is a matrix organization; this can be done directly by creating a matrix reporting structure for employees. However, two organizational structures can aid in horizontal alignment outside of a matrix organization:

1. Centers of Excellence (CoE)
2. Communities of Practice (CoP)

### Centers of Excellence: Remove the Cultural Divide

One element that helps to create a sustainable data and analytic culture within an organization is to establish an Analytics Center of Excellence. In our first book, *It's All Analytics* (Burk & Miner, 2020), Burk and Miner discussed the different types of organizational structures which included:

■ Centered
■ Decentralized
■ Matrix or hybrid structures

Now, one important facet of the CoE is the reporting structure within the organization. In the book, *Building Analytic Teams* by John K. Thompson, there is an interesting discussion on the CoE reporting structure. Thompson argues that the best organizational home for the CoE is reporting directly to the Chief Executive Officer (CEO) or the Chief Operating Officer (COO).

When a CoE reports to the CEO, this typically signifies the priority and importance of the CoE to the organization. Also, this would certainly create strong alignment between the organization's strategic objectives and the projects and initiatives that the CoE will undertake. Additionally, this helps with ensuring that the CoE has the appropriate amount of funding and that corporate project management and change management teams are appropriately involved.

Now, realizing that the CEO is extremely busy and may not have the appropriate amount of time to spend with the CoE, Thompson believes that reporting to the COO is the next best option since the COO has all the corporate functions reporting to them. In addition to being able to help marshal the necessary resources for the CoE, the COO can help facilitate and promote collaboration between the CoE and the various business units as needed.

Now that we have explored the optimal reporting structure for a CoE, where is the worst corporate home for a CoE? We (and Thompson) feel that putting the CoE within an IT organization is probably the worst possible place for them. Why is this the case?

The analytics process is iterative in nature and takes a great amount of creativity and innovation to map specific analytic techniques to business problems. As the analytics team attempts to discover, explore, and investigate different analytic approaches, there will be successes and failures. The team will continue to iterate until a suitable approach is found. Then the team will refine and optimize that particular approach.

Now, if we consider how an IT organization operates, they are typically risk averse and do things in a very structured manner (and for good reason). The creative and interactive elements are, for the most part, nonexistent within an IT organization. Therefore, if an analytics CoE reports to an IT function, they will, over time, pick up and start to emulate the norms and behaviors of the overall IT function. Additionally, IT management will tend to reward the CoE if they are behaving and acting similar to how the rest of the organization acts. In other words, the analytics CoE will begin to draw up detailed plans, change management processes, and overall, will be more risk averse compared to if they were not reporting to an IT organization. The two paradigms comparing how an analytics team operates and how an IT team functions could not be more diametrically opposed.

## Communities of Practice: Knowledge Sharing across the Organization

CoPs are gaining popularity and offer a rich framework within your analytics program. A CoP does not exist within a division, a department, or an operational function. Instead, a CoP exists for the entire organization, and thus may include staff across any function within the organization.

A CoP is a group of people who want to learn, create, and share information about a common topic or domain. The CoP is developed as a framework to facilitate these three principles. In the end, the organization benefits by having these pools of experts interacting and leveraging information on what works and what doesn't work. There are three major types of CoPs that can exist within the analytics program. ***The first type*** is determined by the set of AI and analytics techniques deployed. For example, it could be professionals using visual analytics such as dashboards and understanding the types of business problems these techniques can solve. Alternatively, it could be professionals using advanced analytics and machine learning techniques and understanding the types of business problems these techniques can solve.

***The second type*** of CoP is based on software systems/tools/platforms that can be deployed to solve analytic problems; for example, users of a particular visual analytics dashboarding software platform, or users of a particular machine learning platform or programming language and its application to the organization. ***A third type*** of CoP could be based on functional role – a Marketing CoP or Finance CoP with open membership that allows for cross-fertilization of ideas and knowledge.

Communities of practice are a great way to get people to work together outside traditional roles. It can also groom people for their future roles in the organization. For example, someone outside the marketing department (say data science or finance) could join a Marketing Analytics CoP and they could learn and contribute. They could bring outside knowledge in with a new perspective to problem-solving. And, they could be learning about marketing so that if they wanted to make a career move down the line, they could do so.

## The Power of Straightforward, Clear, Honest Communication

You cannot have a high-performance culture without straightforward, clear, and honest dialogue. Such a culture is one that brings reality to the surface through openness, candor, and informality. This type of dialogue makes an organization effective in gathering information, understanding the information, and reshaping it to produce decisions. It fosters creativity – most innovations and inventions are born from straightforward, clear, and honest dialogues. Ultimately, it creates more competitive advantage and stakeholder value.

> "Honesty and transparency make you vulnerable. Be honest and transparent anyway". – Mother Teresa

Straightforward, clear, and honest dialogue starts when people go in with open minds. They are not trapped by preconceptions or fears. They are not singularly focused on their private agenda. They want to hear new information and choose the best alternatives, so they listen to all sides of the debate and make their own contributions.

## THE GM NOD AND SALUTE

**The GM Nod**: As described by Mary Barra, this is a practice of GM managers sitting in a room, nodding in agreement at steps that need to be taken (their own nonverbal communication styles with an effectiveness which would have made Don Corleone proud), and then leaving the room and doing nothing. This nonformal agreement leads to deep clique and politics. It does not promote finding real solutions to company problems – it promotes suboptimal local wins.

**The GM Salute**: The Valukas Report defines this as the habit of employees going through meetings, with their arms folded and pointing to others, as if to say that the responsibility lay with others, not with them.

The Cobalt disaster cost GM $ billions. It almost destroyed the company. This is an example of the cost of nodding, saluting, and doing nothing.

When people are allowed to speak candidly, they express their real opinions, not those that will please the power players or maintain harmony. Indeed, harmony – sought by many leaders who wish to offend no one – can be the enemy of truth. It can squelch critical thinking and drive decision-making underground. When harmony prevails, here's how things often get settled: after the key players leave the session, they quietly veto decisions they didn't like but didn't debate on the spot. A good motto to observe is "**truth over harmony**". Candor helps wipe out the silent lies and pocket vetoes, and it prevents the stalled initiatives and rework that drained energy.

Informality is critical to candor. Formality suppresses dialogue; informality encourages it. Formal conversations and presentations leave little room for debate. They suggest that everything is scripted and predetermined. Informal dialogue is open. It invites questions and encourages spontaneity and critical thinking.

### JEFF BEZOS ON MEETINGS AT AMAZON

Meetings have a reputation for being time and $ wasters, motivational drainers, and idea destroyers. You should do everything you can to make your meetings as efficient and effective as possible.

Two things we can learn from Jeff Bezos are:

1. **Most people are better thinkers in the AM**. Make sure that you have meetings that require the most brainpower in the morning. Bezos says he goes to bed early, rises early, and schedules "high IQ" meetings before lunch.
2. **Most meetings are pointless. Make them matter**. Mr. Bezos is well-known for his insistence that meetings be productive. To facilitate that, he requires presenters to write a memo, no longer than six pages, that is circulated and silently read at the start of a meeting by everyone present. Mr. Bezos praised the memo process in one of his letters to investors: "Some have the clarity of angels singing", he wrote. "They are brilliant and thoughtful and set up the meeting for high-quality discussion". Employees have said they spend weeks perfecting their memos, a process that sharpens ideas and improves decision-making and discussion.

Reference: *The Wall Street Journal*, Lauren Weber, February 2021.

## Environment for Creativity and Innovation

AI and analytics success commands an informal, nondictatorial atmosphere where ideas can be exchanged freely and openly without the fear of quickly being shut down. You must create an atmosphere conducive to idea creation and experimentation. You want to create a process to vet and test your ideas, but that comes later in the process.

The best way to have great ideas is to have many ideas. You cannot have many great ideas; therefore, some ideas will be bad – you need to create the environment where bad ideas are welcome. Think about children, they are the most creative beings on the planet – they live out of their imagination. What happens as they age? They have ideas that they are told are stupid and most of them shut down. It is a rare person indeed that can keep childlike imagination going. It is rarer that this person is willing to expose those ideas outside their mind for fear of judgment.

> "Innovate. Then innovate some more". – Jeff Bezos

So, what can you do as a leader to maximize creative thinking?

1. Encourage open and informal dialogue, emphasis on "informal".
2. Rid your organization of tyrants and haters at every level.
3. Create an environment that fosters and rewards experimentation.
4. Eliminate the guise of power players and hierarchy. Flatten the organization.
5. Create a matrix environment. Get rid of rigid functional silos.
6. Create a collegial environment.

A common misperception is that the most creative companies are the most innovative and successful companies. Wrong.

Millions of great ideas have never been put into practical use, because of a lack of personal or corporate discipline. You have to have the discipline to convert ideas into reality. Creative enterprises are only successful if they capitalize on the best ideas. To some, this is the boring, mundane, hard work. That is why you need to build your team with multiple players with different strengths. *The best creators are not necessarily the greatest "doers".*

What can you do as a leader to maximize transformation of winning ideas into reality?

1. **Embrace Failure**. A common theme with high tech and innovative companies is that they embrace failure. Failure and innovation are inseparable. You cannot have one without the other. Jeff Bezos at Amazon said: "Embrace Failure. Failure and innovation are inseparable".

2. **Experiment/Test/Validate**. Testing ideas is the key to innovation. There are great statistical methods to test ideas with smaller, less expensive samples. Some of these methods are very much like A/B testing. Much more powerful methods exist. Get everyone thinking about not only new ideas, but leaning to think how they could test their ideas. Once an idea looks like it might work in a controlled environment – get it in the real world. See #3.

3. **Test Your Ideas in the Real World as Soon as Possible**. Marc Randolph (Netflix) says that there are no good ideas, meaning once an idea hits reality, it doesn't live up to the beautiful picture the mind created; therefore, people are afraid to test their ideas in the real world – "They want their experiments to work, and so they do this terrible thing where you keep it in your head, where it's safe, and where it's warm, and where you can embellish it, and it's a great idea, as long as it's all imaginary and in the safety of your head". You move the best ideas into the real world and test them appropriately.

4. **Compensate for Ideas and Testing**. Most people get this wrong. They want to reward the results that turned out to be stars. Yes, we love stars too much. Execution needs to be rewarded, so you get more attempts at bat. Reward the ideas and testing that people do – not results. Build a compensation system that rewards ideas and testing methods – whether they fail or make it big – if the decision-making is sound – you should compensate the people!!

5. **Learn, Document, and Refine**. You should create an interactive learning environment. Document your successes and failures with your analysis of what went right and what went wrong. Discover what better decisions could have been made and why they were not made. Hone the process and get at it – iterate and converge to optimal performance.

## Environment for Decision-Making

Straightforward, clear, and honest dialogue is needed for decision-making, and this is fostered by the environment created for innovation. However, there are some nuances to be considered in meetings and the boardroom. You must add closure to your dialogue. At the end of the meeting, people agree about what each person has to do and when. It is now on record. They have committed to it in an open forum; they are accountable for the outcomes.

The reason most companies do not face reality and carry out effective decisions is that their dialogues are ineffective *or* they do not follow through. It shows in their results. Think about the meetings you have attended: those that were a hopeless waste of time and those that produced energy and great results. What was the difference? It was not the agenda,

> "Good order is the foundation of all things". – Edmund Burke

not whether the meeting started on time or how disciplined it was, and certainly not the formal presentations. No, the difference was in the quality of the dialogue and the commitments to follow through.

Open, honest, and candid communication alters the psychology of a group. It can either expand the group's capacity or shrink it. It can be energizing or energy-draining. It can create self-confidence and optimism, or it can produce pessimism. It can create unity, or it can create bitter factions.

It should be open, tough, focused, and informal. The aim is to invite multiple viewpoints, see the pros and cons of each one, and try honestly and candidly to construct new viewpoints. This dynamic stimulates new questions, new ideas, and new insights rather than wasting energy.

How do you get people to practice open and honest debate if they are used to the games and evasions of classical corporate power plays?

It starts at the top, with the narrative and behavior of the organization's leader. If they are practicing open and candid communication, then others will take the cue. This may take some effort. Leaders tend to have egos and it may require them to stifle natural reactions and muster the emotional strength required to invite disagreement without getting defensive.

The key objective is to drive people's action and behavior toward data-driven strategies and organizational results. Senior leaders must communicate and then demonstrate a new world order of straightforward, clear, and honest dialogue.

You must reward their performance to this end, then others in the organization will model the behavior. To succeed, everybody needs to make the best decisions. That means everybody must be candid in their exchanges. Everyone needs to hear others out. No one person has all the ideas. You need to be able to experiment in an environment of trust. You must be able to make rational decisions and experiment without fear of backstabbing. You must be able to speak what you believe and feel, without fear of losing your job for taking risks. Leading is about trusting people and assuming they are going to do the right thing knowing that sometimes people will disappoint you.

Another thing you must reward is the quality of the decision process and not the business outcome. Many decisions are made with great analysis and decision-making processes and then some external factor kills the idea/decision. Imagine that an excellent marketing plan was constructed to expand a restaurant chain across New York City and the plan bombed. Should the team that put the plan together be fired? Receive no bonus? What if the year was 2020? Do you want to reward people on the outcome or the quality of their work?

Just because you have a bad outcome does not mean you made the wrong decision. Jim Collins recommends analyzing decisions without blame (autopsy without blame). Analyze the facts; look at the process, not just the outcome. We are not saying that you should say "everyone tried hard so it is not their fault" or "everyone did their best so the bad outcome is not their fault". We are saying, "this decision did not result in the outcome expected, it was a failure". Why is this the case?' Assume everyone is innocent, and if the autopsy is such that they followed a sound process, they should not be punished for it. However, if they followed a poor decision process, then they should.

## *Leaders Get the Behavior They Exhibit and Tolerate*

Once you understand social operating mechanisms and the importance of straightforward, clear, and honest dialogue, you understand that no leader who is disengaged from the daily life of the business can possibly change or sustain its culture.

Dick Brown said:

> The culture of a company is the behavior of its leaders. Leaders get the behavior they exhibit and tolerate. You change the culture of a company by changing the behavior of its leaders. You measure the change in culture by measuring the change in the personal behavior of its leaders and the performance of the business.

To shift to an AI and analytics culture, you need to start at the board level. Information needs to be disseminated clearly and opening about the goals and objectives. The investments in time and money that will be required need to be presented clearly and accepted. The patience and contributions the CEO will require from the board will need to be made clear.

> "Art is about building a new foundation, not just laying something on top of what's already there". – Price

If you have already instituted a program that is not working, you need to reset it.

> *"This analytics thing is not for us" is not an option, not embracing analytics is a clear path to extinction.*

You have to find the path forward.

The messaging starts with the CEO; the message must be consistent and clear that the organization will run as a data-driven enterprise to satisfy all customers and stakeholders. Each leader at every level should add their viewpoints specific to their organization. This messaging cascades downward to every layer of the organization. This is not a onetime effort – it is as consistent as a drumbeat, this messaging is constant.

In division or higher-level meetings, leaders present a new way of conducting business and develop the total company picture for all to see. Managers come prepared to explain how their departments fit into the larger objectives. By discussing the entire business and having to focus on the external environment, everyone participating knows more about overall trends, competition, issues, and roadblocks. If they are doing their job to help build a culture of data-driven execution, this information will cascade through the company.

## MANAGEMENT BY OBJECTIVES (MBOS) AND WHY THEY ARE IMPORTANT

MBOs were introduced by Peter Drucker (the father of modern management). He introduced this practice of management as a way to improve organizational performance. In essence, MBO describes a process of defining specific and clear objectives for employees and is designed to create a culture of working toward common organizational goals.

The performance review is largely modeled after the concept of MBOs where a manager agrees on objectives with each employee, and then their performance (and compensation) is assessed against these objectives.

While each department or unit has very specific tasks and obligations, it is important that they see how they connect into the larger picture and how their outputs affect others. The key ingredient that is often missing in organizations is alignment. Mixed signals and misalignment of goals and measurement of success of those goals have to be in lock step or else you get frustrated employees.

## BUT SAM IS THE PROBLEM! MISALIGNMENT OF EMPLOYEE INCENTIVES AND GOALS

An employee was frustrated because their ratings were down on their quarterly rating. This employee was on both a commission bonus and an MBO bonus (Management by Objectives, a management concept framework based on a need to manage business based on its needs and goals).

The employee was given a special assignment at the beginning of the year and told that their quarterly MBO bonus would be heavily weighted toward it. Yet, while every quarter they were given accolades to their leadership, on this special project their MBO bonus was lacking. Every quarter they got the same story from their manager, "I know you have done a great job on this assignment, but Sam wants to know what big deals you have closed?" To which the employee would respond, "but, that is a separate bonus reflected in my commission bonus. We were told that MBO bonuses were long term content, team and pipeline generation, not sales? Why are we double dipping into the commission pot? I was told my leadership on my special project would count heavily toward my MNO bonus and it is not reflected, why?"

The response from the manager would always be: "… need to ask the administrator of your special project to make sure Sam knows". When this was done, the administrator was told by Sam that the employees' MBO was heavily weighted toward the special project and the employee was compensated. This was not true. O, the trouble with Sam. *In frustration, the employee ended up leaving.*

It is absolutely critical to have financial incentives clearly laid out and adhered to or the consequence could be losing the best people. Furthermore, you need to root out leaders who lack integrity.

**Note**: We are speaking a lot about corporate culture and changing corporate culture. However, many cultures are linked hierarchically. Think about geographic cultures – global, country, state, community, social, and family. At the highest level, some norms and behaviors are shared. Then as you move down the chain, each group has its own unique set of identities. We call these "microcultures" and they are present within all organizations, businesses, and public entities. The point is to strengthen the valuable, common ties from the highest level to the lowest level while preserving autonomy and control at the local level.

## The Most Important Thing Leaders Have Control Over – Hiring and People Placement

Control over maybe a little bit of an overstatement. Leaders do not have total control over hiring and placement of people, but they do have a lot of influence. And, comparing that control to the many things that businesses can't control, from the uncertain

> "Great vision without great people is irrelevant". – Jim Collins

state of the economy to the unpredictable actions of competitors, you would think companies would pay careful attention to the quality of the people they hire, especially those in the leadership pool. Human capital is the most reliable resource for generating excellent results year after year. Judgment, experiences, and capabilities make the difference between success and failure.

Yet, many leaders do a poor job in hiring while at the same time exclaiming, "People are our most important asset". There are several reasons for this. *First*, many leaders consider that it's HR's job to hire only competent and capable candidates. In reality, HR cannot fully know the intimate details of the job function, determine proficiency of a candidate's knowledge and skill set, or even know the right questions to ask about problem-solving and experience. Nor can HR assess the "microculture fit" of a candidate to the hiring department.

*Second,* if it is not a direct report to the leader, they may say, "I trust Susan's judgment in hiring her people and so I do not need to be involved". There are two problems with this. Susan may only be thinking about her department and not the organization at large. Susan has her direct set of responsibilities and therefore she is focused on local issues for the current period, not corporate challenges or tomorrow's challenges. It is her leadership that should be thinking about the larger organization and what the organization will need down the road to meet future trials.

Beyond hiring, what does the organization do with poor performance? There are many causes of poor performance. It may be temporary and due to issues outside the organization. It could be an employee whose role has changed and they haven't been properly trained or may not have the aptitude for the new challenges. Whatever the reason, managers and leaders need to make tough choices and remedy the problem immediately. Delaying action normally makes the remedy more difficult and time consuming. It also sends a terrible message to the rest of the organization that leadership is weak and/or indecisive.

You need to identify the root cause. Hopefully, it will be identified as a gap in training or education that can be fixed. Or, alternatively the person can be moved in a new role. If not, leadership must find the best way for both parties to move forward separately.

Sometimes, leaders don't pay enough attention to people because they're too busy thinking about the end game; like how to make their companies bigger, improving margins or more taking market share. What they are overlooking is that the quality of the people is the best competitive differentiator. Overlooking this is short-term thinking. The results probably will not show up immediately, but over time, choosing the right people is what creates that elusive sustainable competitive advantage.

### NO MORE IMPORTANT TASK?

Peter Drucker coined the term "knowledge workers" to refer to people whose main capital is to think for a living. They work with their heads, not their hands, to plan, analyze, organize, test, program, distribute, search, market, or otherwise generally contribute to the transformation of information in the knowledge economy. He said that "increasing the productivity of knowledge workers was the most important contribution managers needed to make in the 21st century".

This is correct and therefore there is no more important task than getting the right people on board and letting them innovate.

If you look at any business that is consistently successful, you will find that its leaders focus intensely and relentlessly on people selection. Whether you are the head of a multibillion-dollar corporation or in charge of your small profit center, you cannot delegate the process for selecting and developing leaders. It is the leader's job.

## The People Challenge

Everyone acknowledges we need the right people in the right jobs to maximize the chances of being successful. Yet so often they aren't. What accounts for the mismatches you see every day? The leaders may not know enough about the people whom they're appointing.

They may pick people with whom they are comfortable, rather than others who have better skills for the job. They may not have the courage to discriminate between strong and weak performers and thus take the necessary actions. All of these reflect one fundamental shortcoming: the leaders aren't personally committed to the people process or deeply engaged in it.

Leaders often rely on staff appraisals that focus on the wrong criteria. Or, they'll take a fuzzy and meaningless recommendation for someone a direct report likes. "Bob's a great leader", the candidate's advocate exclaims. "He's a great motivator, a great speaker. He gets along with people, and he's smart as hell". The leader doesn't ask about the specific qualities that make Bob right for the job. Often, in fact, he doesn't have a good grasp of the job requirements themselves. He hasn't defined the job in terms of its three or four nonnegotiable criteria – things that the person must be able to do in order to succeed. Any leader or hiring manager should be able to answer this question: "What are the three nonnegotiable criteria for this candidate must possess to be successful in this job?"

Most people know someone in their organization who is not performing well. Yet they manage to keep their job year after year. The usual reason, we find, is that the person's leader does not have the emotional strength to confront them and take decisive action. Such failures can do considerable damage to a business. If a nonperformer is high enough in the organization, they can destroy it.

Honest and robust performance may be one of the most challenging tasks that managers and leaders take on. It is hard to be brutally honest with someone. Even harder if you have to separate with a worker with whom you have had a relationship over a long time period. Most people want to form bonds and relationships with the people in their work organization. They want to feel comfortable and that presents another problem. But remember the lessons on fresh starts (see the gray box on page 22, **Lessons from Major League Baseball – Consequences of Moving Personnel**). Oftentimes, a move is very beneficial for the individual and the organization.

Many jobs are filled with the wrong people because the leaders who promote them are comfortable with them. It is natural for executives to develop a sense of loyalty to those whom they have worked with over time, particularly if they come to trust their judgment. However, it can be a serious problem when the loyalty is based on the wrong factors. For example, the leader may be comfortable with a person because that person and they seem to think alike. They may not challenge the leader's opinion, or have developed the skill of insulating the leader from conflict. Alternatively, the leader may favor people who are part of the same social network, built up over years in the organization.

Is it better to know a person's record intimately or hire from an unknown quantity from the outside? This is where your hiring process comes into play. You can be objective about someone on the inside by asking, "Would I hire this person if all I knew was based on their resume and how they would perform in an interview? Can, I contrast the knowledge I get from our process of vetting recommendations versus my own experience with someone I have worked with?" This can be a difficult call.

When the right people are not in the right jobs, the problem is visible and transparent. Leaders know intuitively that they have a problem and will often readily acknowledge it. Nevertheless, an alarming number don't do anything to fix the problem. Ram Charan suggests:

> Leaders need to commit as much as 40% of their time and emotional energy in one form or another, to selecting, appraising, and developing people. This

immense personal commitment is time-consuming and fraught with emotional wear and tear of giving feedback, conducting dialogue, and exposing your judgment to others.

But, the foundation of a great company is the way it develops people – providing the right experiences, such as learning in different jobs, learning from other people, learning candid feedback, and provide coaching, education, and training. If you spend the same amount of time and energy in developing people as you do on budgeting, strategic planning, and financial monitoring, the payoff will come in sustainable competitive advantage.

Most people regard a good leader as one with vision, strategy, and the ability to inspire others. They assume that if the leader can get the vision and strategy right, and get their message across, the organization's people will follow. So Boards of Directors, CEOs, and senior executives are too often seduced by the educational and intellectual qualities of the candidates they interview: are they conceptual and visionary? Articulate? A change agent?

To champion a winning AI and analytics culture, your leadership will need all those prerequisites. But, in addition, your leaders must be hands-on champions of the program. In reality, there's very little correlation between those who talk a good game and those who get things done. You need to get this done, so you must ask the most important question: how good is the person at getting things done?

Inspiring people through rhetoric will not cut it. Too many leaders think that they can create energy by giving pep talks, or painting an uplifting picture of where the business be in a few years if everybody just does their best. The leaders whose visions come true build and sustain their people's momentum. They bring it down to earth, focusing on short-term accomplishments – the adrenaline pumping goals that get scored on the way to winning the game.

Additionally, your leaders need to be decisive on key issues. Decisiveness is the ability to make difficult decisions swiftly and well, and then act on them. Organizations are filled with people who dance around decisions without ever making them. Some leaders simply do not have the emotional strength to confront the tough ones. When they don't, everybody in the business knows they are wavering, procrastinating, and avoiding reality. Organizations are starving for decisiveness.

> "Be decisive. Right or wrong, make a decision. The road of life is paved with flat squirrels who couldn't make a decision".
> – Anonymous

Suppose someone you really like isn't cutting the mustard. Few tough issues are more challenging for indecisive leaders than dealing with people they've promoted who are not performing.

Big speeches without follow-through are meaningless. *Follow-through is the cornerstone of success.* Every leader who's good at executing follows through religiously. Following-through ensures that your people are doing the things they are committed to do, according to the agreed timetable. It exposes any lack of discipline and connection between ideas and actions, and enforces the specificity that is essential to synchronize the moving parts of an organization. If people can't execute the plan because of change circumstances, follow-through ensures they deal swiftly and creatively with the new conditions.

Never finish your meeting without clarifying what the follow-through will be, who will do it, when and how they will do it, what resources they will use, and how and when the next review will take place and with whom. And never launch an initiative unless you're personally committed to it and prepared to see it through until it's embedded in the DNA of the ornamentation.

### HOW TO END A MEETING

Paul Axtel relates important closing points you should do at every meeting (HBR, 2015):

**Check for Completion**: If you move to the next topic too quickly, people will either cycle back to the current topic later or they will leave the meeting unclear or misaligned. You should ask: "Is there anything else someone needs to say or ask before we change topics or adjourn the meeting?"

**Check for Alignment**: If someone cannot live with the decisions being made in the meeting, or the potential outcome of those decisions, you need to ask that person what it would take to get him or her on board. People prefer to be united with the group, and if they aren't, there's a reason behind it that needs to be surfaced. Asking the question, "Is everyone OK with where we ended up?" will surface questions or concerns so that they can be resolved as soon as possible.

**Agree on Next Steps**: Getting firm, clear commitments is the primary way to ensure progress between meetings. In order for a conversation to lead to action, specific commitments must be made. Progress depends on clearly stating what you will do by when and asking others to do the same. To maintain the momentum of any project, nail down specific commitments and deadlines, and then follow up often. The question here is: "What exactly will we do by our next meeting to ensure progress?"

**Reflect on the Value of What You Accomplished**: This is one of the most powerful acknowledgment and appreciation tools. People rarely state the value created by a conversation, and therefore lose a wonderful opportunity to validate both the conversation and the individuals in it.

**Check for Acknowledgments**: Did anyone contribute to the conversation in a way that needs to be highlighted? While you don't want to use acknowledgment and appreciation so frequently that it becomes a commodity with no value, at times someone's questions or remarks do help provide the tipping point that turns an ordinary conversation into an extraordinary one – and that's worth acknowledging.

## Getting the Right People in the Right Jobs

Traditional interviews are not useful for finding the leaders who have the qualities needed to ensure they can execute. Too often, traditional interviews focus on the chronology of an individual's career development and the outline of specific assignments they have had. Interviewers do not usually dig into the person's record to see how they actually performed in previous jobs. How, for example, did they set priorities? Did they include people in decision-making? Can they justifiably take credit for those good financial results, or were they just moving from position to position, one step ahead of calamity?

There are far too many examples of people who have chalked up an admirable record by the numbers at the expense of people and then left behind a weakened organization. They jump ship at the right time, and their successors have to clean up their mess. Even when interviewers check references, they often fail to get the heart of the matter. Scott (one of the authors) has provided dozens of references, and while he has never given a glowing recommendation to someone he considered a poor performer, he has focused more on the strengths of some candidates than weaknesses. Of course, Peter Drucker says you should focus on strength, but the hiring party may have not heard of Drucker. In general, what is the exchange for someone providing a reference? They have no allegiance to the hiring company. They may have some allegiance to the candidate under consideration.

When you interview, you have to create a full picture of the person in your mind based on the things you can learn by probing them. Then you will find out about their past and present accomplishments, how they think, and what drives their ambitions.

Nowhere is candid dialogue more important than in the people process. If people cannot speak forthrightly in evaluating others, then the evaluation is worthless – to the organization, and to the person who needs the feedback.

Most people we see, however, have never received an honest appraisal. It takes courage and emotional strength for those doing the appraisals to be forthright. More often a manager thinks, if I sit down and tell this person he or she has a behavioral problem, that's a confrontational discussion, and I don't want to have it with him or her. Without guidance, practice, and support, moreover, many managers do not have enough confidence in their objective judgments to be critical.

There is nothing sophisticated about the process of getting the right people in the right jobs. It is a matter of being systematic and consistent in interviewing and appraising people and developing them through useful feedback.

## Organizational Environment and People

Culture eats strategy for breakfast.

– Unknown

> People like us, do things like this. That is the defini-
> tion of **culture**. Figure out who the people like us
> are, figure out what the things like this are. And then
> you can make something change or understand how
> the world is.
>
> – Seth Godin

The people process is more important than either the strategy process or the operations process. After all, it's the
people of an organization who make judgments about which
products and services to offer, create strategies based on
those judgments, and translate the strategies into operational
realities. To put it simply and starkly: if you don't get the
people process right, you will never fulfill the potential of
your business.

A robust people process does three things:

1. It evaluates individuals accurately and in-depth.
2. It provides a framework for identifying and developing
   leadership talent – at all levels and of all kinds – that the
   organization will need to execute its strategies today and
   down the road.
3. It fills the leadership pipeline, providing the basis for a
   strong succession plan.

Very few companies accomplish all of these objectives well.
One of the biggest shortcomings of the traditional people process is that it is backward-looking, focused on evaluating the
jobs people are doing today. Far more important is whether
the individuals can handle the jobs of *tomorrow*.

We have seen many people who led business units well,
sometimes even superbly, who did not have the capability to
take the business to the next level. Too often companies wait
until the financial results are in before making corrections in

key leadership positions. By then, the damage is done. The results are lagging indicators; they record the past, and with a time delay to boot.

The heart of execution lies in three core systems:

■ Systems of people
■ Systems of strategy
■ Systems of operations

Driving successful AI and analytics execution is about looking at these three systems independently as well as the linkage between them. It includes making assumptions about the business environment, assessing an organization's capabilities, linking strategy to operations and the people who are going to implement a strategy, synchronizing those people and their various disciplines, and linking rewards to outcomes. It also includes mechanisms for changing assumptions as the environment changes and upgrading companies' capabilities to meet the challenges of an ambitious strategy.

A bad cultural environment is toxic. Stars have other professional opportunities and they will not tolerate a toxic environment for long. They will leave. The organization will be stuck with the mediocre and poor performers who will do just the job with tight lips and "toe the line" only to preserve a paycheck.

The greatest toxicity is an environment that is a tyrannical leadership: one that does not sponsor and promote a collegial and supportive workplace – an environment that is creative, energetic, and has a culture of open dialogue. Where people are afraid to speak what is on their mind, where the lack of open debate stifles the ability to learn and make decisions based on frank truths, stifles sharing of opinions, and even leads to open dissent.

### THE TROUBLE WITH SAM – WE
### CALL HIM RADIO SAM

Sam was a tyrant. He demanded to be heard and he demanded people do exactly what he said – no qualifications or commentary. If he started to receive any feedback, he quickly shut it down. It was so bad that he earned the reputation of **RADIO Sam – he only transmits, he does not receive!**

A successful leader assembles an architecture of AI and analytics based on the organization's ability to execute that strategy. They put in place a culture and processes for executing, promoting people who get things done more quickly and giving them greater rewards. Their personal involvement in the architecture is to assign the tasks and then follow up. This means making sure that people understand the priorities, which are based on his comprehensive understanding of the business, and asking incisive questions. The leader who executes often does not even have to tell people what to do; they ask questions so they can figure out what they need to do. In this way they coach their people, passing on their experience as a leader in educating them to think in ways they never thought before. Far from stifling people, this kind of leadership helps them expand their own capabilities for leading.

## Do This Right Now: A Fulcrum Greater than Culture – Structure

"If Culture eats strategy for breakfast then Structure eats Culture for dinner". – Safi Bahcall

There is little debate that corporate success or failure relies heavily upon corporate culture. However, developing an analytics culture takes time; changing any culture takes time. One of the immediate things that any organization can do is to optimize their structure to improve the odds of success.

If your organization is very small, it is easy to garner an atmosphere of team/shared values – everyone wins together or dies together. If you are part of a biotech start-up with ten people, people work together because it is either everyone succeeds and becomes wealthy or everyone fails and you are out of a job that you have heavily invested yourself in. Your stake is in the outcome of the entire enterprise; the entire enterprise must succeed. Even if you perform very well relative to others, that does not matter because if the ship goes down, everyone goes down. Furthermore, your peers must deliver and therefore you cheer for them; you do everything you can to make sure they succeed because their success is the collective success, your success. With only ten people – everyone is important!

What happens in an organization of 10,000 people? First, you typically have lots to layers, with staff, department managers, directors, senior directors, vice presidents (VPs), senior VPs, and executive VPs. Fancy titles are even created to make people feel more important, because it is easy to get lost in a large organization. Rank matters, rank matters a great deal.

With rank, politics, posturing, positioning, and games ensue. Life becomes a zero sum game, meaning for me to win I have to take someone down. Backstabbing, turf wars, and petty behavior ensue to make me look better. This is a downside of human nature, but it exists as a defense mechanism – the only way for me to win is for you to lose. This creates real problems in many organizations. What is at stake now is my survival, not the organization's survival, so I will forfeit the good of the organization for what is good for me.

For example, suppose everyone in a department knows that their manager, a rising star, is likely to be promoted in the next year and that manager will be naming their replacement. What is the natural behavior during the next year? The behavior is to try to rise above all your peers and the easiest way to rise above your peers is not individual accomplishment. No, it is to undermine all your peers.

As a leader, you need to carefully consider options to mitigate the politics and games in your organization. One thing to consider is providing structure within your organization to promote the good of the whole. It will be highly dependent on the size, maturity, and nature of your organization, but consider one example provided by Safi Bahcall.

Safi suggests that you separate what he calls artists versus soldiers. Artists are the creative types within the organization, the idea creators, scientists, engineers, designers who are responsible for conceptualization. Artists embrace risk – they want to be on

> "For Successful AI Projects, Celebrate Your Graveyard". – Sandeep Uttamchandani

the edge, push the envelope, and develop something radically new. Soldiers are responsible for taking ideas and concepts and turning them into viable products and services. They have practical considerations and therefore are risk averse; they want consistency and control.

Every enterprise has both types of roles; the next structure you can provide promotes freedom for each to do their thing and then come together to wed concept to reality for viable innovation. This comes in three parts. *First,* you separate these camps as much you can in space and systems to allow for homogeny. One example for a good system is compensation – you want to reward these camps very differently – the artists should not be punished for product idea failures that do not make it in the market. Their responsibility is creation. Soldiers are responsible for determining if the artist's creation is commercially viable and the successful launch of the product or service.

*Next,* you need to allow for systems of transfer that maximize fluidity whereby you maintain the best of each group's contribution. *Third,* as a leader you honor each groups' value to the organization. This often does *not* occur in organizations and it undermines the capacity of those organizations to compete. For example, Steve Jobs, version 1.0 – his first tour at Apple ended shortly after he alienated so many, that it became problematic for him to continue as head of Apple. He called the artists "heroes" and the soldiers "bozos". Artists represented 5% of the company and soldiers represented 95%. In his second tour at Apple, version 2.0, a more mature Jobs realized that everyone was needed as part of the team, and thus he became a much better leader. The point is, if you do not need someone in your organization, you should not have them there – if they are there, honor them as key to the organization's success.

## GOOGLE'S QUEST TO BUILD THE PERFECT TEAM

Google wanted to build better teams, knowing that better teams would yield better results. So, initially they thought that the secret might be – "who – what types of people – belongs on the team together". Maybe put friends together or maybe we should group all introverts with other introverts and all extroverts with other extroverts, or maybe we should mix personality types. What they found was that who was put on the team was not the most important thing.
     What mattered most was:

1. People were free and willing to talk up
2. People listened to what they had to say

In the end, this creates psychological safety. You do not have to like the other people in the group, but you do feel that you are free to speak your mind and other people are actively listening to your ideas and opinions

Two important contributors – *no* laptops or cell phones on in meetings.

## Developing an Executable Strategy for AI and Analytics

> Everyone has a plan until they get punched in the face.
>
> – Mike Tyson

Developing a strategy is critical to any business. However, anyone can develop *a* strategy. You want to make sure your AI and analytics strategy is:

1. Solid and that it aligns and supports the market and operational strategies of your organization
2. Adaptable to internal and external forces
3. Designed to be executable by your organization

"Employees at three out of every five companies rated their organization weak at execution – that is, when asked if they agreed with the statement 'Important strategic and operational decisions are quickly translated into action', the majority answered no". – HBR, June 2008

Strategies are worthless if they fail. They are worthless if they never get used, if they are never acted upon. They are worthless if they cannot or will not be executed by the organization's available resources. This is where most companies are failing the promise of AI and analytics. It is lack of action. "Employees at three out of every five companies rated their organization weak at execution – that is, when asked if they agreed with the statement 'Important strategic and operational decisions are quickly translated into action', the majority answered no" (HBR, June 2008). This section is about overcoming these pitfalls.

## Alignment and Support of Market and Operational Strategies

Your AI and analytics program does not exist to "check a box" or provide a nod to a board member that you heard them in a recent meeting. It should be a machine to drive your business objectives forward. It should make your existing processes easier and less expensive, enhance growth, and improve customer experience. It should enable you to launch new initiatives that you would have been unable to implement with it. Your strategy should be built into your culture so that people look at problems in new ways, in more innovative ways.

First, you should start with your existing goals and determine how AI and analytics can support them. If it is operational efficiency that is being sought, what manual processes might be augmented or automated with assistance of machine learning models or visual analytics? If it is producing sales volume, what predictive models might be created to provide more effective target accounts and improve your sales funnel and conversion rates?

This book is not about specific AI use cases. We will provide some references on that in a following section, "Pillars for AI and Analytics Success". The simple point is that your program exists to support other initiatives, not to stand by itself. Some organizations make the mistake of "if we build it, they will come", meaning you create the program in isolation, the business will seek it out to solve its problems with analytic techniques. Instead, you must start with business problems and carefully build the analytics strategy to support the business.

You build the program and your analytic strategies together, in unison. At some point your AI program will become so ingrained within your organization that it becomes your DNA, and at this point, you become a data-driven culture. Nevertheless, you do so by showing the value of being data-driven. Not data-driven techniques looking for a problem to solve. One of the key problems in AI and analytics strategy is that only senior leaders are involved. This approach will lead to failure. You must include the entire organization in the process. Lower level "staff" are the people who have the biggest role and time commitment in implementing the strategic plan. If you do not include them, they will not "own it".

Larry M. Miller, Institute for Leadership Excellence, defines an approach to align levels and leaders of the organization. Summarizing this approach in an abbreviated fashion: Senior leadership is responsible for defining strategic goals, core processes, future culture, and capabilities. Senior leadership writes a design charter and assigns to design teams. The design teams discover the current states, dreams for ideal states, and they convert these into a technical and social system plan that they pass onto the business units and distributed leaders. These business units and distributed leaders assign implementation tasks and teams that create action and accountability plans. They then discuss these at an "alignment conference" where all levels of the organization attend and identify new design requirements. See Figure 2.2, adapted from Larry's work.

Note that strategy often defines the future business and economic performance, but not the means to get there – the future processes, culture, and capabilities. This must be tailored to your unique organization. Also note that strategy execution is too often a vertical, silo-ed, performance review

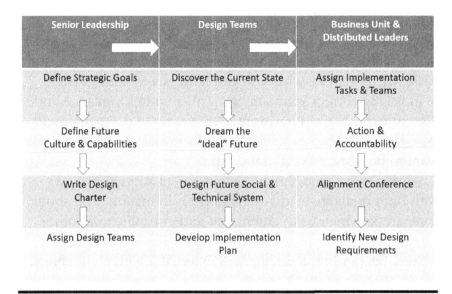

| Senior Leadership | Design Teams | Business Unit & Distributed Leaders |
|---|---|---|
| Define Strategic Goals | Discover the Current State | Assign Implementation Tasks & Teams |
| Define Future Culture & Capabilities | Dream the "Ideal" Future | Action & Accountability |
| Write Design Charter | Design Future Social & Technical System | Alignment Conference |
| Assign Design Teams | Develop Implementation Plan | Identify New Design Requirements |

**Figure 2.2   Strategy alignment for execution. Adapted from Larry M. Miller.**

process and does not create horizontal alignment. We offered some suggestions in a previous section that help with horizontal alignment – "Centers of Excellence and Communities of Practice".

## *Adaptable Strategies*

We love the Tyson quote at the begging of this section because it is so true. As we have said many times in the book – creating a strategy is easy, making it viable in face of internal organization dynamics and external market forces is hard. Sometimes these events feel like "getting punched in the face" and you need to be ready.

What mechanisms will you put in place to adapt your strategy in the event of a strike, losing key leadership positions, or a major

The problem is that strategies are often not "agile", dynamic, and responsive to changes in the landscape.

systems failure? What will you do in a market downturn, a new major entrant in your industry, or a competitive merger that was unanticipated? You cannot prepare for every scenario. Nevertheless, what you can have is a system in place to judicially correct your strategy. This requires vigilance and discernment. You do not want to overreact to a situation and abandon plans that should stay in place. Likewise, you do not want to bury your head in the sand.

At minimum, you should have frequent strategy reviews with both qualitative and quantitative information. You should compare key metrics to attainment and critically account for variances in your plan. You should view the landscape on what is happening internally and externally with competitors, the industry, and the economy.

It is important to engage everyone in the process of executing the strategy – from strategy design teams to deployment teams. Deliberately and systematically, design the system to be "capable" – capable in both the technical systems and the people/cultural systems. Strategy execution must be both horizontal and vertical to create alignment.

Be agile in adapting to external threats and opportunities.

## Executable Strategies

A strategy is worthless if you do not have the resources to execute it. Therefore, the entire planning process should be built around your capabilities and willingness to execute the strategy. Note – *capabilities* AND *will*. Capabilities are financial and intellectual. Will is cultural.

Design your strategies with your capabilities and will in mind. This cannot be overstated. Many times strategies are developed in the boardroom with little input from the rank and file. Furthermore, the leaders who are developing them want to seem greater and more capable to the CEO than they truly are. They bite off more than they can chew so that they can seem like great leaders. And they fail.

## Key Points

1. Strategic planning must include all members of the orga- nization. Those in the lower ranks have to make it hap- pen – because of two key reasons:
   a. They know what is achievable.
   b. They will be accountable if they are part of the process.
2. Capabilities – knowledge and resources are in place or can be attained.
3. Willingness – the culture to support is in place or can be secured.
4. Financial resources are secured that include training.

### FIRE BULLETS, THEN CANNONBALLS

Fire bullets, then cannonballs is a concept developed in the book *Great by Choice* (Jim Collins). First, you fire bul- lets (low-cost, low-risk, low-distraction experiments) to fig- ure out what will work – thus calibrating your line of sight by taking small shots. Then, once you have empirical vali- dation, you fire a cannonball (concentrating resources into a big bet) on the calibrated line of sight. Calibrated can- nonballs correlate with outsized results; uncalibrated can- nonballs correlate with disaster. The ability to turn small proven ideas (bullets) into huge hits (cannonballs) counts more than the sheer amount of pure innovation.

In interviews, Collins has said that when you are firing bullets, you cannot predict which are going to be your big cannonballs in the future. You have to understand up front that some of the bullets will not amount to anything. Not every bullet will become a cannonball. The whole point is the uncertainty; you do not know which bullets will turn out to be a cannonball. So, you have to be firing enough to have some hope so that some will come close to hitting the target.

If you are going to fire a bullet, you have to go about it the right way, fire it well, meaning if you are going to do a test, you do not want to find yourself afterward asking (if the bullet does not hit), "is that because the bullet will never hit OR we did a bad job of it?" If you are going to fire a bullet (experiment), take the right precautions, do the experiment right. Statisticians are great at designing experiments so that you never have to ask these types of questions. Consider hiring one.

"Strategy defines and communicates an organization's unique position, and says that it should determine how organizational resources, skills and competencies should be combined to create competitive advantage". – Michael Porter

It is one thing to say you want to become a data-driven organization that can execute on AI and analytics capabilities. Many organizations have done this and failed? Why? Because they created a strategy without considering the organizational capabilities. It does an organization no good if it creates a beautiful strategy that cannot be executed by the organization.

It is critical that you align the strategy to the organization. This will require effort. If it were easy, everyone would do it and many AI programs would not be failing.

CEOs often underestimate how difficult it will be to execute an AI and analytics program. That has caused many programs to fail. AI and analytics have massive potential. A leader will read and look at programs like Amazon, Apple, CitiGroup, Facebook, Google, JPMorgan Chase, Microsoft, or Salesforce and be inspired by the results. They will get energetic, meet with top leaders, and form a strategy. This strategy will be formulated without regard to or details of **how** it will be executed. Or, the CEO will assign the entire initiative to one of their direct reports, like the CIO, CTO, or COO, to take and initiate the program. We saw these issues in the last section. The CEO and any leader that has had a hand in the creation of the strategy is married to the strategy and this causes a blindness to the difficulty in implementation of the strategy.

Strategy execution is a hot topic in management today. In fact, the Conference Board's recent Survey of CEOs revealed that chief executives are so concerned about strategy execution that they rated it as both their number one and number two most challenging issues. For anyone who has tried to execute strategy, this finding should come as no surprise: it is estimated that more than 60% of strategies are not successfully implemented. The numbers are higher in data-driven strategies, AI, and analytics.

Why does strategy execution so often fail? Because most strategic plans are little more than a series of vertically integrated objectives. But the problem is not objectives, and it is not vertical. It is the "whole-system" and its ability to adapt and align, internally and externally, in fast cycles. In other words, to be agile. The problem is the culture and capabilities of the organization and a process to design and deploy those capabilities.

## LINKING STRATEGY TO OPERATIONS
## FOR COMPETITIVE ADVANTAGE

In 2008, Harvard Business School Professor Robert S. Kaplan and his Palladium Group colleague David P. Norton wrote

*The Execution Premium: Linking Strategy to Operations for Competitive Advantage.* In it they present their management system, which houses six sequential stages intended to help organizations capture what they call an "execution premium" – a measurable increase in value derived from successful strategy execution. They outline six stages in this system:

1. Develop the strategy
2. Plan the strategy
3. Align the organization
4. Plan operations
5. Monitor and learn
6. Test and adapt

Reference: American Management Association article by Ed Barrows.

## Internal versus External Strategies

You will need to develop both external and internal strategies.

**External strategies** are about the marketplace:

1. Who are our customers?
2. What products and/or services do we offer them?
3. What are the needs of shareholders or owners?
4. How do we position ourselves versus our competitors?

**Internal strategies** are about capabilities within the organization to support the external strategies, specifically:

1. Do we currently have people working that can support our external strategies? If not, can we recruit, outsource, or train those capabilities?

**Figure 2.3   Alignment of business direction and execution.**

2. Do we have the infrastructure in place to support our external strategies? The IT systems? The organizational structure? A partner ecosystem?
3. Do we have the capital, the cash flow, financial resources to fund the strategies?
4. Can we reinvent our processes to support new strategies?

You have to align the internal strategies to support the external strategies. A graphical representation adapted from Lawrence M. Miller is shown above in Figure 2.3. You can see the circular nature of the internal and external forces at work. Externally, leaders

"Plans are worthless, but planning is everything". – Dwight D. Eisenhower

are specifying the products, markets, and competitive positioning for the business. Internally, they are addressing the current state and the needed state (capabilities) to execute these strategies. As capabilities rise, the business can grow and expand.

As you execute, your focus will change. All the while, you will have to dynamically change your external and internal strategies to adapt to changing forces.

Internal and external strategies should be developed in concert as they are integrally intertwined. And, this needs to be done in a cascaded fashion, starting with the highest level, the board or CEO level. Then to the executive VP, Senior VP, VP level … and then pushed down into the divisions, departments, and units.

## Two Faces of Internal Strategy

Some examples of internal strategy were just listed. We can categorize these as technical or social. Technical strategies include organizational structure, policy, IT systems, and operational processes. Social systems include strategy around people. Of course, these categories overlap and interact. Making these designations helps in a few ways, but most importantly because the social systems are:

1. More difficult to change
2. The mechanisms to influence them are much more subtle
3. They take longer to influence
4. Mistakes made with them are less likely to be quickly detected
5. Influenced with changes in personnel
6. Heavily influenced by external social norms and movements

## Assessment and Transformation in Strategic Planning

Assessment and transformation are two major parts of strategic planning. Assessment is gathering information and analyzing the current state of the unit. This will be at various levels – the entire organization, division, department, unit, and work group. You analyze the unit's (or work group's) culture and capabilities to accomplish specific goals.

Transformation is taking the existing capabilities (current state) and mapping requirements needed to get it to the future (desired state).

## *Barriers to Transformation*

Much of what has been presented is straightforward; it is basic, elementary. So why isn't it done? Why is it not common practice? In fact, "Employees at three out of every five companies rated their organization weak at execution – that is, when asked if they agreed with the statement 'Important strategic and operational decisions are quickly translated into action', the majority answered no" (HBR, June 2008). This is a little dated, but from our experience, we do not believe it has gotten better; in fact, we think it has gotten worse.

Lawrence M. Mills lays out common problems and solutions. Based on our conversations, we think this directly translates into executing your AI and analytics program.

**Problem**: Only senior leaders are involved. The plan is not "owned" by those who must implement the plan.
**Solution**: Engage everyone in the process of executing the strategy. Form strategy design and deployment teams.
**Problem**: Strategy often defines the future business and economic performance, but not the means to get there – the future processes, culture, and capabilities.
**Solution**: Deliberately and systematically, design the system to be "capable" – the processes and social systems.
**Problem**: Strategy execution is too often a vertical, silo-ed, MBO process and does not create horizontal alignment.
**Solution**: Strategy execution must be horizontal and vertical to create alignment.

**Problem**: It is too often not "agile", dynamic, and responsive to changes on the landscape. Not viewed as a whole system.
**Solution**: Be agile in adapting to external threats and opportunities.

### COVID LESSONS FOR STRATEGIC PLANNING: ADAPTABILITY AND RESPONSIVENESS

The COVID epidemic wrecked many businesses. Some did not survive. Some are still in the ICU and may never recover. Some are doing better than ever.

Obviously, there are many factors that contributed to these differences in results that are outside the business's power – industry, size, capitalization, etc. However, some differences can be explained by corporate structure and decision-making. Strategic plans and operating plans that were constructed to be adaptable for the diagnosis of a need to change quickly separate many outcomes. Was there any slack built in for resources – financial and staff resources? Did the strategic plan incorporate any failover or recovery mechanisms?

Adaption is the key to survival in biological systems as well as organizational systems. It is not the strong that survive – it is the adaptable that survive. COVID should teach us that your strategic plans should be quickly adaptable and responsive to changes in your organization's environment.

# Implementing/Operationalizing Your AI and Analytics Program

Once you have aligned your AI and analytics strategy to your organization's capability to execute it, there are two things a leader has influence over when it comes to getting results for your analytics program. First is **developing the strategy**. What does "Developing the Strategy" mean? – Basically what do we want to accomplish and how do we go about accomplishing it? The second is the ability to **execute that strategy**. Which is more difficult? Execution is the hard part. Execution requires a change in human behavior and it is hard enough to change our own behavior, much less someone else's behavior.

Which of the two has more educational offerings? What do MBA programs offer – education on developing strategy or execution of the strategy? When you look at executive seminars and conferences, there are many for strategy development. Massive Open Online Courses (MOOCs) have exploded over the last few years and there are hundreds on developing strategy and very few that offer courses on executing strategy.

CEOs often underestimate how difficult it will be to execute an AI and analytics program. That has caused many programs to fail. AI and analytics have massive potential. A leader will read and look at programs like Amazon, Apple, CitiGroup, Facebook, Google, JPMorgan Chase, Microsoft, or Salesforce and be inspired by the results. They will get energetic, meet with top leaders, and form a strategy. Their strategy will be formulated without regard to or details of **how** it will be executed. Or, the CEO will assign the entire initiative to one of their direct reports, the CIO, CTO, or COO to take and initiate the program. We saw these issues in the last section. The CEO and any leader that has had a hand in the creation of the strategy is married to the strategy and this causes a blindness to the difficulty in implementation of the strategy.

## Getting Everyone on the Same Team

Everyone on the team (the entire organization) has to know and be committed to the goal of "becoming a data-driven company empowered by AI and analytics literacy and

technology". Becoming a data-driven company empowered by
AI and analytics literacy and technology becomes the corporate mantra. It is the corporate initiative. People know it, they
live it. They know it is not a "flavor of the month" slogan.
We have no doubt, leaders and frontline staff should have no
doubt – if you fail in your mission to become driven by data
and analytics, you will not last long in the new world.

Leadership also defines how the organization will specifically succeed with AI and analytics. They define specific
goals for their AI and analytics programs. These goals may
include gaining market share, increasing revenue or margin,
customer retention, or cost containment. They are developed
among all analytic stakeholders that represent the business
stakeholders, the AI and data stakeholder, and IT. We present idea generation in our *It's All Analytics* series, *Part III*,
where we discuss linking business initiatives to AI and analytics capabilities (*It's All Analytics – Part III* is not expected
to be released until 2023).

The next step gets more personal – **how** employees can
make these initiatives happen.

## Getting People to Play Their Position – "How" to Execute

Once everyone knows what the goals are, they then have
to know **how** they will help achieve the goals. Considering
the football team metaphor, everyone has a position to play.
The corporate goals are very important for the frontline staff
to know, but more importantly, they have to know how they
have an impact upon the organization. They may have influence over some corporate goals and not others. It is management's responsibility to align their department's goals within
the corporate goals based on their operational responsibility. Then within the department, they must break down the

department goals by specific work function. The best way to do this is a popular management strategy called "Objectives and Key Results" (OKRs). This technique starts with the organization's highest level of objectives and key results (metrics to be tracked). Once these are in place, every level of the organization will track their activities upward to map their functions and activities to those objectives.

In a hierarchical organization, you might have division OKRs align to those corporate OKRs. Then departmental OKRs aligns to the division OKRs. Then units align to division and then finally an individual's OKRs align to their units OKRs. Some benefits of this process are organizational alignment, clarity, and objectivity. Once an individual has their objectives defined, they understand how their analytic work results contribute to corporate goals.

## Knowing the Rules of the Game and Keeping Score

Keeping score is more difficult than it may seem. The goal is to win the Super Bowl. You will know once you get there if you succeeded, but getting there is difficult. You need to break it down and it is typically best to work backward – you have to get to the Super Bowl, therefore you have to win a divisional championship, therefore you have to win so many games, therefore you have to outscore your opponents, therefore players must execute their positions, and coaches need the right game strategy and call the right plays, and practices have to be run efficiently and effectively.

> "If you're not keeping score, you're just practicing". – Chris McChesney

The winner of the Super Bowl and the winner of single games are easy metrics to track. Tracking individual performance is much more difficult. Some players will never touch the ball, yet they significantly influence the score. You have to determine individual scores for each player in their relative position. More about this in "Nuances and Difficulties in the Game".

## Holding Players Accountable

We have already spoken about the importance of feedback and the difficult decisions of leadership and management. Once players know their role in the game and how they impact the corporate goal, it is critical that they are compensated for how well they execute their personal plan. Furthermore, they should be rewarded to the level they advocate for the program overall. Are they going through the motions or are they staunch believers? The ideal is zealots that deliver!

### THE IMPORTANCE OF CONTRACTS

Good contracts make for a good understanding. This means agreeing to what both parties are going to do. When you sign a contract, you hope you never have to revisit it. Nevertheless, if you do, it provides clarification and an opportunity to resolve the issue and maintain the partnership. You can get back on track.

A contract is an understanding of what two trustworthy parties are agreeing to. You would never enter into a contract with an untrustworthy party, so the spirit of the contract must be sound – both parties expect to benefit from the relationship. It provides clear expectation of the role and responsibilities of both parties.

Finally, the proof of a good relationship is that if you ask either party who benefits the most from the relationship, each party would reply that they do!

## Nuances and Difficulties in the Game

We just highlighted four straightforward practices in operationalizing your corporate strategy for AI and analytics:

1. Getting everyone on the same team
2. Getting people to play their position – "How" they contribute to execution
3. Knowing the rules of the game and keeping score
4. Holding players accountable

Does this sound complex or difficult? Most people would say no. Is it common? We know it is not and not embracing these key factors to executing analytics programs is the reason for failure in most analytics programs. Why? We highlight a few of the reasons.

### That's Not My Day Job!

What if your organization had no corporate goals or key strategies, would your people still be busy? Yes. They have day jobs. Most organizations don't free up any time for employees when they add on additional responsibilities. They just add work on top of it. Good employees will try to do it all; sometimes they burn out as a result. Bad employees will either just not do one or the other. Any employee might decide to find work elsewhere if there is a better opportunity.

Let's suppose you have a good employee and they are committed and trying to do it all. They are doing a good job with their daily work activities and attending special education for the AI and analytics initiatives. They are in training when their boss calls about a customer support issue, the storm hits. They know the training is very important. Customer support is urgent. What happens when the urgent meets the important – which wins? The urgent. That is the correct action. Customers have to come first in this scenario. The storm is the urgent, today's customer requirements. The important is often, what are tomorrow's customer requirements? Both are often complicated by external forces.

> "What kills the grand strategy? It is not because leaders are incompetent or defiant. It is the real work".
> "If you ignore the urgent, it can kill you today. It's also true, however, that if you ignore the important, it can kill you tomorrow". – Chris McChesney

Is there anything you can do! Yes! First, you need to have a minimal number of corporate goals or strategies. We think your data initiatives and your AI and analytics programs should be your number one priority. Nevertheless, in our new world, certain industries have their own priorities. You must decide. However, you need to minimize the number of activities that impact employees' time and energy so that they can focus on the important whenever they can. You need to minimize the storm, the fire drills in whatever way you can, including adding some fat to your organization. You need to add this fat so that you can cover an employee's day job while they attend training without constant worry that things are falling through the cracks while they are away. You need to add fat to free up some time for creative thinking about ways for them to support the initiatives. You need to free up some of their time so they can be vocal advocates and mentors of data and analytics literacy.

## COVEY AND MCCHESNEY – THE FOUR PRINCIPLES OF EXECUTING STRATEGY

The Covey Leadership Center studies leadership and management practices. It attempts to distill its research into common principles. Stephen R. Covey and Chris McChesney outline four key principles to operationalizing strategy:

1. **Principle 1 – Focus**. The Covey Leadership Center recommends one to three corporate goals at any one time.
2. **Principle 2 – Act on the lead measures**. Lead measures come before the desired outcomes. More on this follows.
3. **Principle 3 – Capturing the bet**. Keep a compelling scoreboard.
4. **Principle 4** – Create a cadence of accountability.

## Special AI and Analytic Activities Become Part of the "Real" Job Over Time

When you are beginning your AI and analytics program, there is a lot of education and preparation work. Some of these activities include:

1. Kick-off campaigns at the corporate level with
   a. What the program is and means to the company
   b. Why it is important
   c. How it will affect personnel and the company
2. Leader's education and messaging specific to their departments
3. Departmental meetings tailored to the function and role of the department and how the program will be rolled out and function within the group and how individuals will be incented to participate
4. Appropriate education courses
5. Selection of projects

To say the least, there will be a lot of time and energy invested. A natural response to all of this is, "I have a day job and I cannot take time out from it to do all this". But, this is the "Real Job". As a leader, you must be prepared for this reaction. That is why focus, clarity, and alignment of incentives are so important.

Change is difficult and you must embrace the challenge of launching this major program. However, one thing that will happen with time is that these analytic initiatives will become part of the real job. It is important to communicate that "the way we have worked in the past will disappear – we will be functioning as a **data-driven, analytics company**".

# *Chapter 3*

# The Six Foundations for AI and Analytics Success

The loftier the building, the deeper must the foundation be laid.

**– Thomas a Kempis**

There are six foundations that form the success of your AI and analytics program. They are interrelated and nuanced. They are visually represented in Figure 3.1.

Simple descriptions are as follows.

## Business Knowledge

Business knowledge describes the intimate and deep understanding of the operations and critical success factors of your business. What factors contribute most to the success or failure of the enterprise? This includes an intimate knowledge of past, current, and future states of your business. Which core capabilities led to organizational successes, and the lack of which capabilities led to organizational failures? What are the anticipated needs for success in the future?

DOI: 10.4324/9781003175759-3

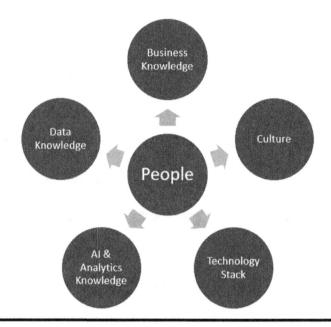

**Figure 3.1    The six foundations of the success of AI and analytics programs.**

# Data Knowledge

Data knowledge starts with the understanding that data is a reflection of process. So, in a way, data knowledge is an extension of business knowledge – the deep understanding of all business processes. Next comes the capture of data to represent realities in the business – what your business is doing and what the results are. In between, the organizations must understand the types and structures of data, how it is collected, combined, and cleansed, and how it will be used.

# AI and Analytics Knowledge

Since data is a reflection of process, the business can use that data to understand the interrelationships of inputs and outputs. How is this variable related to that business result? If I change this part of the process, what is the result? Based on history, what should I expect next year's demand to be? If I enable my organization with interactive visual dashboards, will they make better decisions? Can I build a machine learning model to predict what will happen if I manipulate all of these inputs? Can I create "what-if" scenarios and thus see different models that provide trade-offs? Can it tell us the inputs that will optimize our margin?

These are the types of questions leaders can answer by combining these first three foundations.

One key component of these forms of knowledge is "literacy" – specifically, data and analytics literacy. AI and analytics program success require many in the organization to have a deep understanding of and literacy in these topics. Furthermore, you cannot build a culture without people speaking the same language. Therefore, everyone must have a basic literacy of your business, data, and analytics. This is an important example of how these six foundations are interdependent.

## Technology Stack: Architecture, Platforms, Systems

To turn business, data, and analytics knowledge into results effectively and efficiently, you need to design the right data and analytics architectures. You need to purchase and develop the right technologies.

## Culture

Culture has been one of the four principal focuses of this book – people, culture, strategy, and execution for leaders and decision-makers. As stated, "Organizational culture is the shared values, customs, traditions, rituals, behaviors, and beliefs shared in common by the members of that organization". We have spoken a great deal about culture. Culture has a major impact on your program's success as it influences the reception of knowledge and the use of that knowledge.

In this book, we have provided insights on how leaders affect culture, and the idea that structure and culture may be equally important to innovation.

## People

The reason that "People" is in the center of Figure 3.1 is that people influence everything: who you hire, train, nurture, promote … influences everything. Your people are your organization. That is the reason we have spent so much time on this foundation.

Our focus in this book has been primarily on two of these six foundations for AI and analytics program success – people and culture and the structure and processes that support them. We have also emphasized strategy and execution. These are the hardest elements to get right and implement. These are the elements that leadership, from the CEO through all levels of leadership and management, must be involved in to ensure success.

You will need the other four foundations. You will need data and analytics knowledge/literacy, data architecture, and the technology to support your analytics/AI architecture. Finally, it is crucial you develop your use cases and target your AI and analytics efforts.

We dive much deeper into these six foundations in our **It's All Analytics** series. This series is written to help define your specific AI and analytics strategy, specific roles and architecture for your organization, data and analytics

"Before anything else, preparation is the key to success". – Alexander Graham Bell

literacy, ethical AI, and how AI and analytics are being applied in various vertical industries across a maturity continuum. The series is divided into three parts:

- Part I: *Data, AI and Analytics Knowledge* (book released in 2020)
- Part II: *Organization Design, Data Architecture, Business to Action, AI Ethics, AI and Technology Design* (book released in late September 2021)
- Part III: *Linking Business Initiatives to AI and Analytics Capabilities* (maturity spectrum) (book to be released during 2023)

In summary, all six foundations are necessary for AI and analytics success. People and cultural challenges are the hardest to get right. You also have to execute, so you need to create your strategy with everyone involved, as everyone needs to be responsible in its execution. Finally, don't worry about getting it 100% correct the first time. Planning is meaningful in that it clarifies and educates, but all plans must be abandoned or altered as internal and external environments shift. Be a hands-on leader that is willing to experiment, fail, and learn. Encourage and reward that through the organization. Good luck!!

## Material That Contributed to This Book

We wanted to make this an executive book and avoid official citations, but we should point out many useful references that we used in the construction of this book and you may consider exploring.

*4th Generation Management* by Brian L. Joiner
*Barbarians to Bureaucrats: Corporate Life Cycle Strategies* by Lawrence M. Miller

*Building Analytics Teams: Harnessing Analytics and Artificial Intelligence for Business Improvement* by John K. Thompson

*Confronting Reality: Doing What Matters to Get Things Right* by Larry Bossidy and Ram Charan

*Execution: The Discipline of Getting Things Done* by Larry Bossidy, Ram Charan, with Charles Burck

*Good to Great* by Jim Collins

*Loonshots: How to Nurture the Crazy Ideas that Win Wars, Cure Diseases, and Transform Industries* by Safi Bahcall

NewVantage Partners Releases 2021 – there are lots of culture and more references...

*The 4 Disciplines of Execution* by Stephen R. Covey and Chris McChesney

*The 7 Habits of Highly Effective People* by Stephen R. Covey

*The Game-Changer: How Every Leader Can Drive Everyday Innovation* by Ram Charan and A.G. Lafley

*The Leader's Guide to Change Management: Creating and Sustaining a Dynamic Organization* by Lawrence M. Miller

*The Power of Focus* by Jack Canfield, Mark Victor Hansen, and Les Hewitt

*Whole System Architecture: Beyond Reengineering: Designing the High Performance Organization* by Lawrence M. Miller

*Winning* by Jack Welch and Suzy Welch

# Index

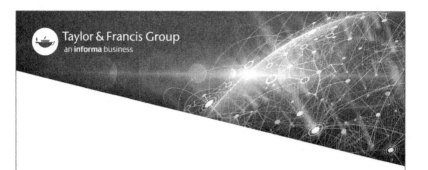

Printed in the United States
by Baker & Taylor Publisher Services